BICESTER

A POTTED HISTORY

MATTHEW HATHAWAY

AMBERLEY

In memory of Ann Hathaway

First published 2023

Amberley Publishing
The Hill, Stroud
Gloucestershire, GL5 4EP

www.amberley-books.com

Copyright © Matthew Hathaway, 2023

The right of Matthew Hathaway to be identified as the
Author of this work has been asserted in accordance
with the Copyrights, Designs and Patents Act 1988.

ISBN 978 1 3981 1707 5 (print)
ISBN 978 1 3981 1708 2 (ebook)

British Library Cataloguing in Publication Data.
A catalogue record for this book is available from the
British Library.

Typesetting by SJmagic DESIGN SERVICES, India.
Printed in Great Britain.

Contents

Acknowledgements

As always, my greatest thanks go to Bicester Local History Society and its members for their wealth of knowledge and vast supply of old photographs. I would particularly like to thank Sally James and Pat Snelson for their help, encouragement and expertise.

I would also like to thank Mark Lawrence and his staff at the Oxfordshire History Centre. They provide some fantastic resources and I encourage anyone interested in local or family history in Oxfordshire to pay them a visit.

Introduction

Bicester is built on a bed of Great Oolite limestone, laid down over 450 million years ago, topped with a layer of Cornbrash rubble stone, formed in the Jurassic Period over 150 million years ago. This geology would go on to influence the appearance of Bicester over the years through the limited range of building materials it supplied. It also contains evidence, uncovered through research at nearby Kirtlington Quarry (worked for cement by the Oxford Portland Cement Co. from 1907 to 1929), as well as other sites, of the region's prehistoric past.

The deep limestone layers were formed in the warm, shallow seas when the area was slightly north of the equator, before plate tectonics moved it a long way further north. The fossil record indicates an abundance of corals, ammonites, crinoids, sea urchins and

The quarry face in 1923 clearly shows the layers of rock and sediment.

molluscs. Dinosaur fossils in the upper layers, including those of Jurassic crocodiles, megalosaurus and stegosaurus, have been discovered locally.

To the south of Bicester lies a band of Oxford clay, forming wet and heavy soil. This is especially evident in the low-lying wetlands of Otmoor.

Eventually prehistoric man came along. From the Mesolithic period onwards, the area slowly became more settled. Initially with hunting and transit camps, these became more permanent as people began to grow crops and keep animals. They could also begin to find and use the available local materials to create the first substantial homes and have objects to keep within them that did not need to be portable. Stone could be extracted from the Cornbrash to build with, and the Oxford clay could be used for pottery.

People became more acquisitive, and trade developed. Religious and tribal beliefs thrived, and burial rites developed. By the Bronze Age wealth began to be symbolic and representative.

Iron made it possible for weapons to be stronger than the copper and bronze ones that had come before, leading many a young warlord to compete with other tribal chiefs as the land became more and more violent. Settlements became heavily protected and fortified.

Trade and coinage had also developed though, and the advances in technology and trade made obvious our large resources of gold, iron and tin, which led to one inevitable conclusion. The Romans were coming.

Invasion and Occupation

Despite its Roman-sounding name, Bicester is not a Roman town. However, we can trace its history back to one of the earliest settlements found anywhere in Roman Britain.

A few miles to the south of Bicester, just outside the village of Wendlebury, lies the site of Alchester, once the largest town in Roman Oxfordshire and, for a very brief period, one of the major military bases in Britain. Its location on an important Roman crossroads was significant for its development as a base, which evolved into a town. While Akeman Street is, in all probability, Iron Age, the main east–west road through Alchester was marked out by Roman surveyors and is precisely aligned with Graven Hill and Tackley Ford.

The main fortress was constructed in around AD 43, as evidenced in part by the remains of a military granary, which was very typical of the Roman army's sites. Shortly afterwards a 4-hectare annexe was added to the 10-hectare fortress. Oak

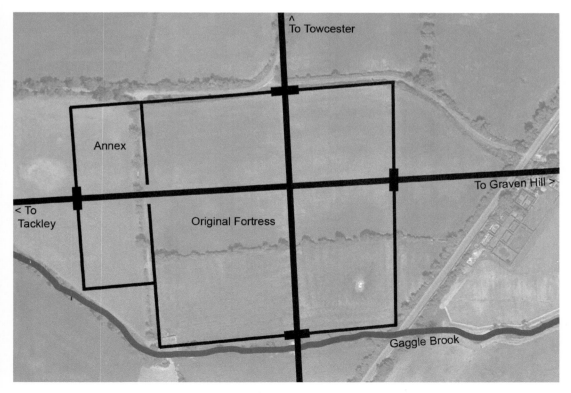

The layout of the fort as it sits in the modern landscape.

gateposts were recovered from excavations in 2000, which were dated to autumn AD 44 or spring AD 45, making them the earliest dated timbers from anywhere in Roman Britain.

Inside the fortress, drainage ditches were excavated together with timber-lined water supply ditches, which suggests that Alchester was one of the earliest sites in Britain to benefit from a flowing water system. The water was taken, by means of a waterwheel, from Gaggle Brook, which runs through the southern edge of the site.

Foundation trenches for timber-framed buildings have been discovered on multiple occasions, and extensive excavations in the western part of the site revealed evidence of barracks. These typically consisted of units of two rooms, one at the front for storage and one at the rear for cooking and accommodation for eight men. The barrack blocks at Alchester were very long, which may indicate that the occupants were legionary rather than auxiliary.

An abundance of weaponry and equipment has been found over the years, including spear and javelin heads, horse armour, and parts of shields and helmets, all suggesting that the Alchester garrison was heavily armed.

The relationship between the invading force and the native population doesn't seem to have been a hostile one. The discovery of sheep bones from small, Iron Age-style animals shows that the army were sourcing food from local farms. Further interaction with the indigenous population is evidenced by a wine strainer made by a British craftsman, which was found in a drainage ditch at the fortress. Additionally, a range of Iron Age coins were located, suggesting trade with the local communities.

We can tell from archaeological finds what life at Alchester may have been like in general, but there isn't much we can tell about specific people. However, there is one individual whose life has been well illustrated by discoveries from the Alchester site. In 2003, the broken remains of a tombstone of one of the inhabitants were found on the site. From the text on the tombstone we can reconstruct some of the man's life story. His name was Lucius Valerius Geminus and he was born in north-west Italy. He took part in the invasion of Britain and retired before the Alchester fortress was abandoned by the Roman army. Since he would have served at least twenty-five years in the army, and Alchester only functioned from AD 43 to AD 55–60, he must have joined at its previous base in Strasburg, which means he would have fought around Frankfurt, the Isle of Wight and Colchester, before retiring age fifty. Veterans commonly retired to an area close to their former base.

Alchester was eventually abandoned by the Roman army, mainly because of the lack of a navigable river and the site's tendency for flooding. The army had left the site by AD 60, but there was still much activity up to the late fourth century at least, as evidenced by the range of coins recovered from the site. Alchester evolved into a town of a respectable size, occupied by retired soldiers, their dependants, and the camp followers who provided services to them. They formed a large enough community to take over the former fortress and transform it into a town. Town walls were constructed around AD 290. Excavations have shown that, except for the bath house, the fortress buildings were made of timber, whereas the town was built of stone. Finds suggest that the town of Alchester remained occupied until the sixth or even seventh century.

The remains of Lucius' tombstone are now held by the Oxfordshire Museum.

It isn't clear why the residents of Alchester left the established town there and moved north, but their choice of a new location, on the banks of the River Bure, suggests that better agriculture and food production may have been the driving factor. Whatever their reasoning though, they founded their new settlement, which would eventually grow into the Bicester we know today, in the area that would become known as Crockwell, where St John's Street now runs. Traces have been found of a Romano-British settlement in the area, with Anglo-Saxon finds showing a settlement further north, which spread southwards as the two grew into one.

There is a natural spring in Crockwell that flows into the river and the name Crockwell, or 'cross by the well', indicates that there was a religious site in the area too. This was likely a cross that stood under a thatched roof in an open space where the local people could gather and hear missionary preachers tell the story of the Gospel. One of these itinerant preachers is said to have been Birinus, the bishop who, according to one theory, gave Bicester its name (Birincester). Another theory suggests that the original name (Bernecestre) means 'fort of Beorna', an Anglo-Saxon warlord. Both spellings of the name, and other versions too, crop up on official documents and there is no specific evidence that favours one theory over the other.

The Romans had built a road heading north from Alchester to Towcester. Today Queen's Avenue and Buckingham Road follow the same route, but back when Bicester

The River Bure, shown here in the 1980s, still meanders its way through the town, though today its more of a stream.

began it would have been a long-neglected track across open countryside. Just north of where it crossed the river, a trackway developed that branched off to the south and ran along the side of the river to Wretchwick, roughly where Manorsfield Road and Chapel Street are today. The Saxon settlement developed along this track.

As the settlement grew, they built a mill further downstream, where the entrance to Priory Lane is today. Its location took advantage of a natural split in the river that allowed them to control one channel to power the mill while the other channel kept the river flowing. The two channels rejoined further south, creating a small island.

At the northern end of the island a shallow stretch of the two channels created a natural fording point, where Causeway is today. This ford gave access to the land on the other side of the river where more dwellings began to develop along a track that later became known as The Street. This ran through the area now occupied by the Church of the Immaculate Conception and Hanover Gardens.

Eventually the local thane, or lord, built his house at the southern end of The Street, where Old Place Yard is today. Its previous name of Old Palace Yard refers back to these early times. This probably followed the Viking invasion of AD 912 when the existing settlement was supposedly attacked and destroyed by the Danes. Some people rebuilt, others moved further south, and the focal point of the settlement shifted to the area around the ford.

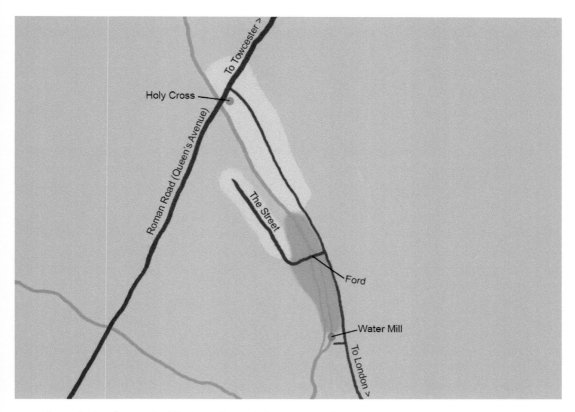

The early development of the town focused along two roads.

Relatively recent discoveries of Saxon burials in both Saxon Court (just off Chapel Street) and around the Church of the Immaculate Conception show that burial grounds were set up on both sides of the river, but we don't know if both sites were in use at the same time or one site finished when the other was started. It is likely though that the first burials on the west side of the river coincide with the founding of a church on the patch of higher ground where St Edburg's Church stands today, right next to the road that led to the lord's house.

2

Medieval Development

Before the Norman Conquest in 1066 Bicester was owned by Wigod of Wallingford. Then it was seized by the Normans and the land was given to Robert d'Oilly, who held it as two manors, Bicester and Wretchwick. Wretchwick was later separated from the main estate, leaving what we know today as Bicester Market End. Robert d'Oilly was also given the city of Oxford and the manor of Middleton Stoney, where he chose to build castles.

The manor of King's End was part of Bignell until it was obtained by the Bedfordshire nunnery of Markyate Priory in around 1150. The priory exchanged some land with Bicester Priory in the early thirteenth century, which may explain why the town centre sits so close to the manorial boundary.

Robert D'Oilly gave the manor of Bicester to Miles Crispin as part of his daughter Maud's marriage dowry. Miles then sold it to Gilbert Basset shortly before his death in 1107. By 1154 Gilbert was dead and had been succeeded by his son, Thomas, who held the manor until he died in 1180. It then passed to Thomas' eldest son, Gilbert, who endowed part of it to Bicester Priory when he established it in 1183.

Basset coat of arms.

The remainder of the manor eventually passed to Gilbert's daughter, Eustachia, whose second husband was Richard de Camville, the son of Gerard de Camville, who owned the manor of Middleton Stoney. Eustachia was dead by 1215 when her only daughter, Idoine, was taken into the king's custody and her wardship was granted to the Earl of Salisbury. She later married the earl's son, William de Longspee, who was formally granted Idoine's inheritance when she came of age in 1226. From then the manor followed the same descent as Middleton Stoney until 1597, when William Stanley, Earl of Derby, sold a 9,999-year lease on the estate to thirty-one of his tenants for £750.

The earl later sold the freehold of the manor to trustees of the leaseholders. In 1605 Thomas Clements, one of the two nominal purchasers, tried to claim the manorial rights and profits of the estate, but it was decided that these belonged to all the leaseholders. So, a bailiff was brought in to manage the manor on behalf of the leaseholders and it became known as the Bailiwick of Bicester Market End.

In the eighteenth century the estates of the Clements family were passed on to Thomas Coker, of King's End, and Edward Turner, of Ambrosden. Edward Turner then attempted to turn some of the leaseholds into freeholds to obtain more votes in the 1754 county election.

By 1816 the Cokers and Page-Turners were the largest lessees of the bailiwick. The Page-Turners tried to claim to be lords of the manor of Market End, but this was unfounded since they didn't own the whole of the estate. However, in 1902 and 1913, Bicester Urban District Council managed just that by purchasing the manorial rights, and all the shares in the bailiwick, from the lessees.

Longspee coat of arms.

The earliest records relating to any church in Bicester date back to 1106 when William, the Elder, witnessed a deed granting the Hermitage of St Cross at Muswell to the Church of Missenden. It states that William was a priest but makes no mention of the church he was associated with. Some of the oldest stoneworks in St Edburg's Church, such as the triangular headed arch on the north side of the nave, show that there was a church on the site as far back as the Saxon period.

William is assumed to have been the priest there and 1104 has been adopted as the official date when the church started. However, there is some belief that it started much earlier, maybe as early as the seventh century after St Birinus had converted Cynegils,

The triangular-headed Saxon arch may be the oldest part of the church.

King of the West Saxons, near Blewbury. Before that the site may even have been a pagan or Roman religious site, as is often found to be the case in other places in the country.

Sometime in the early twelfth century, the new lord of the manor, Gilbert Basset, had the Saxon church developed into a larger structure by adding a chancel and transepts, and possibly a central tower. There is evidence in the stonework above the chancel arch that the wall did crack under the weight of the central tower, but it's not clear whether this happened during construction and stopped the tower being built, or whether the tower had been completed and stood for some time before the structure failed.

The present-day church is dedicated to St Edburg, but there is no proof that this was always the case. In fact, there is some evidence that suggests it may have been originally dedicated to St John the Baptist. It was likely then changed to St Edburg after Bicester Priory (dedicated to St Edburg and St Mary) took over control of the church. This is also the reason why the parish church in Stratton Audley is dedicated to St Mary and St Edburg.

The south aisle of St Edburg's Church, built in the thirteenth century, was the first extension to be made to the church while it was under the charge of the priory next door. The arches and pillars are a good example of the Early English period and are mirrored in the stonework that frames the outside of the south door. The decoration is a lot more intricate around this side of the church, but when you look closely at the stonework you'll find several pieces of reused stone, implying that it was done as cheaply as possible.

Many of the gravestones were removed in 1945.

When the Basset family made the priory responsible for the church and its management they retained the patronage of the church, which was then passed down with the manor of Market End. In the thirteenth century the manor was held by William de Longspee, who was responsible for extending the chancel of the church to the size it is today.

In the fourteenth century, the north aisle was added, and the chapel on the north side of the chancel. Today this area is the vestry and choir vestry, but originally it would have been the lady chapel dedicated to the Virgin Mary. A small chamber was built above the east end of the chapel to accommodate the parish Sexton, which was accessed through the door in the north-east corner of the building and up a spiral staircase.

After the Reformation, Lady Chapels fell out of favour and started to disappear altogether in the 1670s. It was then decided to turn this chapel into a schoolroom for the young men of the parish gentry, as well as a few boarders who lived with the vicar and his family. The arch into the chancel and the screen separating it from the north transept were both blocked up and a doorway was cut into the north wall between the two windows. The Sexton's room became the school library, which included several chained volumes.

When the church was remodelled in 1862 the schoolroom was removed, the doorway was walled up and the arch and screen were reopened. The upper room was later removed, along with the staircase, leaving the door in the corner of the building opening directly into the vestry.

In the early fifteenth century, the tower was built at the west end of the nave. It stands 22.8 metres tall with a battlemented parapet and four decorative pinnacles at the top. The stonework around the top includes two large stones that were originally altars used within the church. The tower consists of four chambers: the ground floor opens into the nave through a 9-metre-tall arch; the floor above this is the belfry where a small window in the north wall looks out over the churchyard; above this is a small chamber that houses the clock mechanism and provides some sound insulation between the bellringers below and the bell chamber above; and at the top is the bell chamber, which is almost as tall as the ground floor level. Today the bell chamber contains a peel of eight bells plus a Sanctus bell. The latter was purchased in 1955 in memory of Reverend Walter O'Reilly, who always took a very keen interest in the bellringing society that used the church bells during his incumbency. He even drew up an official list of bellringers' rules in 1939, which is still displayed in the belfry today.

The final piece to be added to the church building, a two-storey porch, came around the same time as the tower. The upper chamber originally housed the parish clerk, but later this chamber was used to store the four large chests that held the parish registers. As part of the 1862 renovations the chamber was removed and the chests were then stored in the main body of the church, where they can still be found today. Two of the chests bear the dates of 1630 and 1668, and they are still used by the church, though the records they once held are now deposited at the Oxfordshire History Centre.

The church's interior has gone through even more changes than the building itself. Originally it would have been one big open space with a compacted earth floor, but eventually benches were added, and these slowly evolved into pews.

Then, on Saturday 3 August 1765, the tower was struck by lightning during a storm. The lightning travelled down through the fabric of the building, damaging any metalwork it found on its way, including all the leaded stained-glass windows, the bells and the weathervane. Contemporary accounts tell of the church being left 'full of smoke, accompanied with a suffocating sulfurous stench'. The cost of repairing all the damage done was too much for the small town to handle all at once. The structural repairs were completed, but the destroyed stained-glass windows had to be replaced with plain glass, as this was the cheapest and quickest solution. The replacement of the pews with new Georgian-style box pews was largely funded by having families buy their own pew. Lastly, the bells were repaired and rehung in 1766, that work alone costing £47.

As the box pews were mostly privately owned, they were often kept locked by the owners and could only be used by them. In practice this meant that many services had people standing around in whatever space they could find while some pews were left completely empty. As the town grew this made the problem even more acute until eventually several merchants and new residents petitioned the church for permission to build seating galleries in the side aisles, above the existing pews. These went ahead, all privately funded, and were accessed via an external staircase at the eastern end of the

The church's interior, as it appeared in 1849.

south aisle, which went through a doorway built into the window. The petitioners then paid to raise the wooden pulpit (then located in the centre of the nave) up on a platform so that the vicar was still able to preach from above the congregation.

This image, produced in 1849, shows that the galleries, pews and pulpit were still in use eighty years later, but by then space was once again at a premium. Reverend John Watts was the vicar at St Edburg's from 1843 to 1881 and his Sunday services would regularly have a congregation of around a thousand people, so something had to be done.

By 1862 the church had raised and borrowed enough money to completely refit the interior, introduce gas lighting and heating, and complete some necessary repairs to the roof. The refit included removing the galleries and box pews, replacing them with more space-efficient open pews, replacing the old wooden pulpit with a new stone one, and replacing the cheaply repaired medieval window frames with new stonework. The windows still had clear glass in them, but all of them were replaced with stained glass memorial windows over the next few decades. These are the windows that can be seen in the church today.

Church interior after the Victorian refit.

Today's church, with modern lighting, underfloor heating and no pews.

The most recent of the stained-glass windows is a memorial to Charles Adrian Keith-Falconer, who lived in the Garth. It was installed in 1921 at the western end of the north aisle.

The most famous of the windows was designed by Sir Edward Burne-Jones. It is in the south transept, where the doorway accessing the galleries used to be, and depicts the angels of Faith, Hope and Charity. It was installed in memory of Thomas and Mary Tubb, who died in 1847 and 1840 respectively, and their children.

However, the oldest stained glass in the church today is believed to have survived the 1765 lightning strike and is the only complete example of medieval glass still in the building. It is a small window above the priest's door in the chancel and depicts an angel blowing a trumpet. It may even date back to when the chancel was first built in the thirteenth century, but no evidence exists to confirm this.

The Augustinian Priory of St Edburg and St Mary was founded in 1183 by Gilbert Basset, the then lord of the manor and grandson of the Gilbert Basset, who had built the parish church a few years earlier. It consisted of a prior and eleven canons, the number of Christ's disciples.

The priory was endowed with lands and buildings around the town and nearby parishes, including 180 acres of land, two mills and a quarry at Kirtlington, 300 acres of land at Wretchwick, and 135 acres of land at Stratton Audley, Graven Hill and Arncott. It also held a mill at Clifton and had farms let to tenants in Deddington, Grimsbury,

Above left: The Burne-Jones window.

Above right: The medieval Angel window.

Waddesdon and Fringford. Although these properties were extensive, they seem to have been poorly managed as the priory never gained much income from them.

The land given by Gilbert Basset to found the priory was chiefly made up of his own manorial estate and house. The main precinct occupied the site now known as Old Place Yard. It had a gatehouse at the northern entrance, where Chapter and Verse House stands today. The old Basset manor house was converted into the priory accommodation, with a new church being built at its northern end.

Excavations in 2011 uncovered the chancel of the church underneath Bryan House, with the nave extending across Priory Lane and under the car park in Old Place Yard. The church was substantially bigger than the parish church nearby. It was built around 1200 and enlarged around 1300, at the same time as the Purbeck Marble shrine to St Edburg was constructed inside. The shrine may have been the gift of the priory's patron at the time, Hugh de Lacy, Earl of Lincoln.

The south side of the church was linked by a cloister to the quadrangle of the house containing the refectory kitchens, dormitory and prior's lodgings. The priory farm

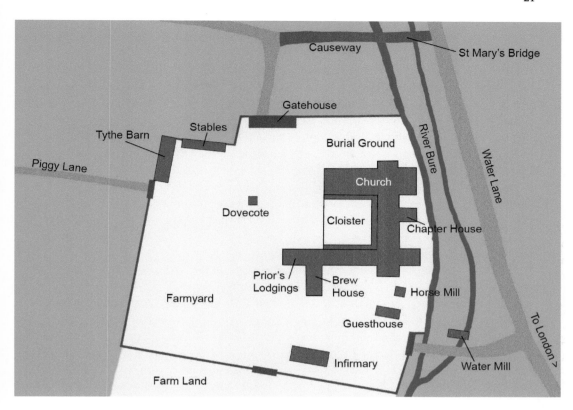

Above: A plan of the priory in its heyday.

Right: Residents in Priory Lane often dig up remnants in their gardens.

buildings lay in the area where Dove Court now stands, with a gate opening onto Piggy Lane where the cemetery is located today. In the south-eastern corner of the site, next to Priory Lane, is thought to have been a guesthouse where any visitors to the priory would have been accommodated. The house, now called the Old Priory, was built on the site of this guesthouse, using recycled materials from the priory after its destruction.

Just to the north of the guesthouse was the priory's mill, which was designed to be driven by a horse walking in a circle around the millstone. The town's watermill, located in the same area, may also have been used by the priory, though it seems rather extreme to have two mills working simultaneously to feed just twelve monks.

As well as the guesthouse the priory also included an infirmary, built somewhere on the southern side of the enclosure. Within this 'Sick House' the monks provided what care they could for the local population. The priory's records state that in 1453 the building was assigned as the residence of the retiring prior as, by then, it had been superseded by St John's Hospice.

Since the priory was never very rich, it was among the first to be closed in 1537. The value of its land and property then amounted to £176 a year. Following its surrender to the king, the priory church was demolished by Simon Harcourt, the sheriff of Oxfordshire, who somehow managed to rescue the shrine of St Edburg from destruction and relocated it to his own parish church in Stanton Harcourt, where it can still be seen today.

St Edburg, the patron saint of both Bicester Priory and the parish church, has always been a bit of a mystery. There have been several Saxon saints bearing the name, often also spelt 'Eadburg', but it is impossible to know for certain which is the saint of Bicester.

Old priory stable buildings, pictured just before they were demolished in the 1960s.

The seventeenth-century dovecote was renovated in the 1960s and probably stands on the foundations of the priory's original one.

It was thought for many years that our saint was St Edburg of Winchester, as depicted in the Victorian banner still displayed in St Edburg's Church. She was the daughter of King Edward the Elder and granddaughter of King Alfred the Great. We know her fame spread far and wide as she is also depicted in a stained-glass window in Pershore Abbey, Worcestershire, but it is more likely that our saint was more local. The village of Adderbury (which takes its name from 'Eadburg's burg') would have likely been named after a lady of high standing in the community, rather than a nun from far down south.

St Edburg of Bicester may have been a daughter of Penda, King of Mercia, who, although pagan himself, had several children who were Christians. Another possibility is that she was the daughter of one of Penda's sons, Wulfhere, who became the first Christian king of Mercia. She could also have been a daughter of Frewald, another local prince. It is generally agreed that this Edburg was born in Quarrendon in the seventh century and was the sister of Edith, with whom she founded a nunnery near Aylesbury. She died around AD 650.

Above left: This Victorian church banner depicts the patron saint of the church, then believed to be Edburg of Winchester.

Above right: What remains of St Edburg's shrine stands in Stanton Harcourt church today.

We don't know where she was originally buried but her relics were eventually brought to Bicester Priory, where many pilgrims came to her shrine and to visit her holy well. Pilgrims were led out of the priory precinct via the Piggy Lane gate and directed to follow the track along until they came across a small spring. They then had to follow the course of the water westwards until it joined a larger stream coming from the north. Then they could follow the route of the larger steam back up to its source, which was St Edburg's Well. Plotting this on modern day maps shows the well was located next to Greenwood Drive, by the entrance to Avon Crescent. There is little sign on the surface of a spring there today, but it is reported to have been dried up since Georgian times.

Over the years the low-lying marshland around the ford became more and more liable to flooding and, as this formed the main access to the priory, the monks quickly had the ford replaced with a bridge (known as St Mary's Bridge) and the road over the marsh built up into a causeway, giving the road its name today.

A licence for a market in Bicester was granted to William de Longspee in 1239 by King Henry III. This was followed in 1252 by a licence to hold a three-day fair on the feast of St Edburg (18 July). Local crafts and skills included leather working and saddlery, rope

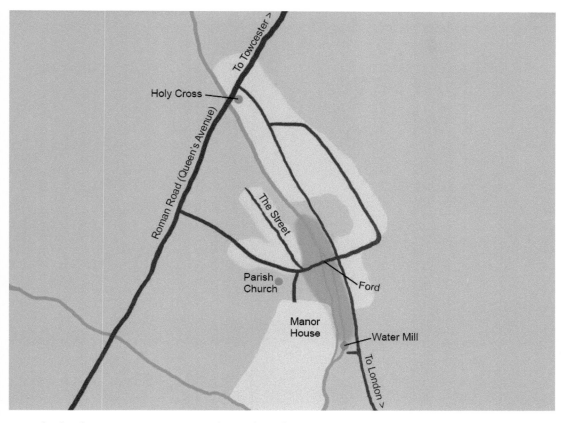

The developing town starts to spread away from the river.

and sack making, basket weaving, straw plaiting, wool combing, as well as lace making and brewing.

A licence for a Monday market and a three-day fair on the feast of St James (25 July) in King's End was granted to St John de Worthe of Bignell in 1377. Normally markets would not be set up within 5 miles of each other, but there is no record of the lord of Bicester protesting the infringement so competition must not have been an issue. After 1464 there is no record of the King's End market.

Weekly markets continue to be held in the town today, though they now take advantage of the pedestrianised Sheep Street rather than Market Square. Cattle and livestock markets continued in Sheep Street and King's End until public health concerns forced them to be relocated to a purpose-built Cattle Market in Victoria Road. This opened in May 1910 and continued to be used for many years before being left derelict and ultimately getting converted into a car park in 2005.

In 1355, most likely prompted by the Black Death, which had spread through the area just a few years earlier, Nicholas Jordon was granted a licence by King Edward III to build a hospital in Bicester for the relief of the sick and poor. This became known as St John's Hospice and was located where North Street is today.

Bicester's weekly market in 1962.

The last cattle market in Sheep Street, 1910.

Opening the new cattle market site in Victoria Road, May 1910.

As the village continued to develop and grow, the convenient supply of water from the river meant that the road running along the side of the river was more desirable for craftsmen and manufacturers. Brewers, alewives, cloth-makers, drapers, butchers, bakers and blacksmiths all moved in, while the residents moved further west onto a new road that spurred off from the existing road next to the hospital and headed south before turning west to rejoin the old road at the junction with the causeway.

On the other side of the river, The Street slowly became abandoned as the residents moved to cottages and farmsteads that developed along a new road that ran from the church up to the old Roman road and would later become King's End and Church Street.

The crossroads at the eastern end of the causeway became a focal point for traders selling their wares. This developed even more when an inn called The Swan was built on the corner where Ambrosden House now stands. It opened with John Fletcher as its first landlord and the area outside quickly began to develop into a fully established marketplace. Then, in 1441, Robert Brooke was granted a market licence by King Henry VI.

'Know ye, that out of consideration of the good services which our dear servant, Robert Brooke, render to us, we and our special grace grant to him a piccage, stallage, boothage and tollage with the assize of bread and beer to our new market below the town to Burcester when all the profits which duly belong to us for which we are informed no account has been given, for the said Robert or his deputy to have, enjoying thence such fees as shall belong to the same paying to us thereof the annual sum of 6s 8d.'

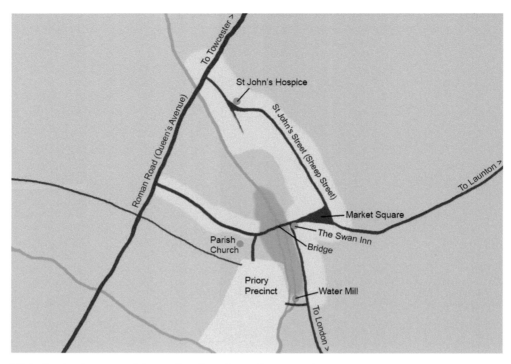

With the development of the marketplace the modern town layout starts to appear.

No. 51 Market Square was built in the late sixteenth century and is one of the oldest buildings in the town.

This may have replaced the earlier licensed market, or it may be that this was the start of the cattle and sheep markets in Bicester and the previous market trade continued unaffected. Either way, local tradesmen began to replace their temporary market stalls with more permanent structures, and over time these evolved into shops and dwellings, giving us the enclosed layout of Market Square that we have today. Some of the oldest surviving buildings in Bicester can be found in Market Square.

This development in trade also led to the growth of properties on the road that came down from the hospital and joined the eastern end of the marketplace. Eventually this became known as St John the Baptist's Street, after the hospital, when the old road running along the side of the river became disused and the main thoroughfare changed. This is what we know today as Sheep Street, from when it took its name from the sheep markets that were held there. The tapered width of the road also comes from its market heritage.

This old window, hidden away on the side of No. 51 Market Square, has seen better days.

3

Tudor Money and Stuart Upheaval

After the dissolution of the priory in 1537 all the priory's lands and property were seized by the Crown. The main priory estate was then granted to the Duke of Suffolk, who, in turn, sold it to Roger Moore for £505. Roger then set about converting the old priory buildings into a family home for himself, his wife, Agnes, and their three children, Thomas, Mary and Elizabeth.

Roger died in September 1551 and Thomas then inherited the estate. Thomas was a Gentleman Pensioner to Queen Elizabeth, serving in her troop of personal bodyguards for many years until he was killed on service in Ireland on 10 March 1574. It was he who supposedly hosted Queen Elizabeth's visit to the town.

As Thomas died without an heir the estate passed to his eldest sister, Mary. She married Michael Blount and the estate then passed down through the Blount family until it eventually found its way into the possession of Sir William Glynne.

This memorial to Roger Moore originally marked his burial place under the floor of St Edburg's Church.

William was educated at Jesus College, Oxford, taking his degree in 1656, and served as Member of Parliament for Caernarfon in 1660 and 1661 before being made 1st Baronet of Bisseter on 20 May 1661. He was High Sheriff of Oxfordshire in 1668 and served as deputy lieutenant for Oxfordshire from 1688 to his death on 8 September 1690.

The estate then passed down through his two sons until his younger son, Sir Stephen Glynne, 3rd Baronet, sold the manor to Sir Edward Turner in 1728. He also sold the manor of Ambrosden to Sir Edward in 1729. Edward was made 1st Baronet of Ambrosden in 1733 but died in 1735 and was succeeded by his son, Sir Edward Turner, 2nd Baronet.

The 2nd Baronet was only sixteen years old when he inherited the estate and title from his father, studying law at Balliol College, Oxford, at the time. He married Cassandra Leigh on 8 September 1739, and they went on to have five children: Elizabeth, Cassandra, Gregory, William and John. He was a magistrate for some years and eventually became a Member of Parliament, representing Great Bedwin from 1741 to 1747, Oxford in 1754, and Penrhyn from 1761 until his death in 1766. Both Edward and Cassandra are buried in the chancel of St Edburg's Church near a large marble monument that is dedicated to their memory.

Edward's eldest son, Gregory Turner, inherited the estate and title upon his father's death, and then in 1780 he also inherited the estate of Battlesden Park, Bedfordshire, from his aunt, the Honourable Judith Page. One condition of the inheritance was that he adopt the name Page, and from then on the family name became Page-Turner. The estates were then passed down through the Page-Turner family until the last parts were sold off in 1930.

At the same time as Bicester Priory's lands were being seized by the Crown and given to the Duke of Suffolk, the lands belonging to Markyate Priory in Bedfordshire were also seized, including the manor of King's End. We don't know what happened to ownership of the manor in the intervening years, but in 1582 John Coker purchased the manor, then known as 'The Nun's Place' from Edward Denton and Ralph Spyer. It consisted of six cottages, 400 acres of farmland, 100 acres of meadow and 200 acres of pasture.

The Coker family moved into the manor house soon after, renamed it Bicester Hall, and it was handed down through the generations until another John Coker, the great-great-great-grandson of the original John Coker, had the house demolished and replaced in the 1790s. It then became known as Bicester House. This house was later remodelled after a fire in 1819 destroyed large parts of it, giving us the building we see today. It remained in the Coker family until 1978.

But it wasn't just the manor house that evolved over the years, the estate as a whole also developed as various pieces were sold off or gifted away for various uses. The first changes we know of happened in 1790 when the grounds around the house were redesigned to suit the new manor house being built. This involved demolishing the cottages in King's End that backed onto the gardens, relocating the residents to new cottages built on Oxford Road, and blocking off the road that ran from King's End to Crockwell, where Queen's Avenue now runs.

Outside of the manor house grounds, most of the estate consisted of Home Farm, with its farmhouse in King's End opposite the present entrance to Bicester House, and its fields extending south along Oxford Road and west along Middleton Stoney Road. But this land

Above: Licence granting the estate to John Coker on 1 December 1582. Now kept in the Oxfordshire History Centre.

Left: Coker coat of arms.

The Georgian Bicester House that replaced the old hall, as it appeared before a fire destroyed much of this south-east elevation.

The front elevation today, following the 1819 remodelling, faces King's End.

made up most of what was sold while the Cokers still owned the estate. Indeed, all that remains today is the farmhouse itself.

First, a small patch of land next to Oxford Road was leased in 1908 to build a nursing home. This was later donated to the trust that managed the home. Then, in 1929, land further down Oxford Road was sold to Bicester Sports Association to provide facilities for their rugby, football, hockey, cricket and rifle clubs.

When Major Lewis Coker died in 1953, Bicester House and the remainder of the estate were inherited by a niece, Denise, Lady Kilmarnock and another relative. But Major Coker's widow, Margaret Coker, was allowed to remain in Bicester House until her death in 1978.

During this time a trust was set up to manage the estate. One of their major sales was the land behind Home Farm farmhouse, on which was built Bicester Health Centre in what became known as 'Coker Close'.

Around the time of Margaret's death, the trustees of the Coker Trust sold just over 2 acres of field at the back of Bicester House gardens to the Hanover Housing Association. Hanover built sixty-nine flats for old people and called the development Hanover Gardens.

Following Margaret's death, the pace at which buildings and land were disposed of increased. Lady Kilmarnock broadly divided up the property into two plots: Bicester House and several acres of formal gardens, plus Bicester House Cottage, coach house, and walled kitchen garden in one plot; the other was Upper Home Close and Foy's Cottage.

Bicester House and the rest of that plot were sold for about £110,000 to a Mr Michael Barker, of Souldern, in early 1979. Within a fortnight, Bicester House and gardens were back on the market and sold for a reputed £89,000 to Mr and Mrs Michael Smith. The other properties were sold off individually. The walled kitchen garden was sold to Leyward Development Company, who sold it on to a development company in Oxford called MCM. They were the builders of the three large, detached Georgian-style houses that now stand just off Queen's Avenue.

Lady Kilmarnock then put the Upper Home Close plot, extending to about 7 acres, up for auction in November 1979. A garage owner, Mr Peter Brewer, paid £114,000 for the land and tried to develop it for housing.

In February 1981 he won an appeal against Cherwell District Council's refusal of planning permission. The appeal heard views from townspeople that the Coker family had not wanted Upper Home Close developed for housing and had deliberately planted it with trees to preserve the land. But it decided that the development would not affect Bicester House, a Grade II listed building, the public had no rights of access over the land, and that tree preservation orders would be put on many of the trees.

So, with planning approval, Mr Brewer tried to develop the site but was thwarted in talks with Cherwell District Council over the price they wanted him to pay to gain vehicle access from Manorsfield Road. Eventually he pulled out of talks and sold Upper Home Close to Bovis Homes, who went on to develop what is now Hunt Close. They also gave the public footpath access from Queen's Avenue through to Manorsfield Road.

Lady Kilmarnock also sold 12 acres of farmland to Bicester Sports Association to extend their sports facilities. A large portion of this sports land was later sold to developers

Charterhouse McGregor for a Tesco superstore and other retail outlets, and the whole site is now occupied by Bicester Village.

Meanwhile, Mr and Mrs Smith allowed several charitable fêtes to be held in the grounds of Bicester House and their front gate was never closed. But, as property prices rose, the value of Bicester House naturally increased too. Several development companies approached the Smiths over the purchase of Bicester House and gardens for the building of retirement flats. Eventually they sold to Bovis Retirement Homes, who declared they would spend about £500,000 renovating Bicester House while converting it into flats and building retirement cottages.

On 11 September 1526 King Henry VIII is supposed to have stopped overnight in Bicester on his way from Winchester to Ampthill in Bedfordshire. It is unclear where he would have stayed, but he would probably have visited the shrine of St Edburg in the priory church and so may have been accommodated by the monks there for the night.

A few decades later Queen Elizabeth is rumoured to have visited the town during the early years of her reign. She came as the guest of the Sir Thomas Moore, who was then living in what was left of the priory.

Cromwell House, which would have been thatched when Oliver Cromwell bedded down here.

Then, almost a century later, sometime during the English Civil War, Oliver Cromwell is supposed to have stayed in Bicester while his Parliamentarian forces were encamped in the area. It is believed that he stayed in the building on the south side of Market Square that now bears his name – Cromwell House.

In around 1600 the marketplace developed even more with the building of a town house. This originally consisted of a single room, raised up on wooden pillars with a staircase leading up to it and a clock mounted in the eastern gable with a bell hung above it. The ground floor was completely open. Further works were done to it in 1622, and then in 1686 the ground floor was closed in with walls around to provide the market traders with some secure storage space. At the same time an open-fronted structure was added to the side. This was known as The Shambles and formed a covered market area, mainly for butchers to use as a slaughterhouse and retail space.

Both buildings were well used and formed a focal point of the market and the town for many years. Such a focal point in fact that, when Corn Law riots broke out in 1826, the buildings were targeted by the rioters and were completely destroyed. The clock and bell from the Town House were salvaged and the bell found a new home on the workhouse when it was built ten years later. It now hangs in the grounds outside the Garth.

The Town House and Shambles, as it looked in 1820.

4

Georgian Gentrification

In the latter years of the seventeenth century and during the first half of the eighteenth century a family of craftsmen named Hemins lived in Bicester.

Edward Hemins was the town clockmaker and gunsmith who supplied a clock to Islip Church in 1707. His son, also called Edward, eventually went on to succeed his father in the family business. Their tower and grandfather clocks are fine pieces of craftsmanship and many still survive today.

Edward Hemins Jr added bell founding to the business in the late 1720s. In following the occupations of gunsmith and clockmaker he was already skilled in the art of casting brass and gun metal, and bell metal is very similar to the latter. Their foundry was in Bell Lane, giving the road its current name.

The earliest Hemins bells that we know of date back to 1728. In that year they supplied one to Preston Bissett and a ring of five to Wootton Underwood. The following year they supplied bells to Oriel College and All Saints Church, in Oxford, and cast bells for Ardley, Broughton Castle, Hook Norton and Piddington.

In 1730 Edward supplied a bell to Edgcot, in Buckinghamshire. The inscription on it is the earliest one we know of where he uses the spelling 'Bister', as any surviving inscriptions from before that always have the spelling 'Bissiter'.

In 1731 he cast a bell for St Clement's Church, Oxford. Then, in 1732, he cast a ring of five bells for Wootton, as well as one for Waterperry and one for Stowe House. That same year he also cast the most significant of his bells, at least as far as Bicester is concerned. It was cast for the Town House that stood in the middle of Market Square and was used as a call bell and clock bell there until the building was destroyed in 1826. Today it hangs in the grounds of the Garth and, as well as the founder's mark, it bears the inscription 'R. Walls, R. Maynard, Overseers. E. Hemins. Fecit 1732'.

Over the following twelve years he cast bells for many churches in the local area. On 28 May 1743 the furnaces of the Hemins bell foundry were used for the last time when Edward cast a bell for Ambrosden Church and a small clock bell for Caversfield House. He died the following year and was buried in St Edburg's churchyard on 8 April 1744.

The Crown Hotel, which once stood on the site of the Sheep Street entrance to Crown Walk, was built in the late seventeenth century and became one of two large coaching inns operating a coaching service from Bicester in the nineteenth century, the other being the King's Arms Hotel on Market Hill.

In the 1840s the Towcester and Oxford Royal Mail coach left the hotel each evening at 6 p.m. for Middleton Stoney, Brackley and Towcester, and then returned to Bicester before setting off for Oxford at 8 a.m. the next morning. It was also possible to hire a range of carriages and carts from the hotel, which were kept in stables at the side of the building.

The Town House bell now hangs outside the Garth.

As well as accessing the stables, the archway on the right also gave access to the Corn Exchange. This was located behind the hotel and hosted many events in the nineteenth and early twentieth centuries, the annual Hunt Ball being one of the highlights.

Henry King bought the hotel in the early 1840s and lived there with his family until his death in 1872. He and his partner, Samuel Beesley, started a coach service to Oxford in 1844 that left the hotel at 9 a.m. every day and travelled via Wendlebury, returning from Oxford at 4.45 p.m. The success of this service led to them extending the route to Brackley in 1847, when the coach would leave Brackley at 7.50 a.m., call in at Bicester at 8.50 a.m., and then reach Oxford in time for the third-class train to London (this was still a few years before the railway came to Bicester). It would then leave Oxford at 4.50 p.m., just after the arrival of the 2 p.m. train from Paddington.

After Henry died, Mark Rest took over the hotel and ran it for several years until he was declared bankrupt in 1889 and was forced to sell it. During his time at the hotel, he established a name for himself within the local hunting community for his excellent

The Crown Hotel is seen here in 1904.

catering skills. He regularly provided the dinners for the Bicester Hunt balls and meetings that were held in the Corn Exchange.

Sometime around 1921 the hotel's ballroom was converted into a cinema. In the days before the Regal Cinema opened in 1934 this was the town's only cinema. Unfortunately, it only lasted for twenty-two years. The cinema was gutted by fire on 4 July 1943. Residents in Sheep Street were terrified that the fire would attract the attention of German bombers, but it did not, and the building later reopened, reverting to its original use as a ballroom.

The hotel was eventually demolished in 1965 to make way for a new Tesco store. During the demolition it was revealed that the building had started life as a two-storey building with a side entry and cellar. But sometime in the early 1800s a third floor was added to the front by altering the roofline and building a new façade.

In 1724 a large fire broke out in Water Lane (now Chapel Street) and quickly spread across the whole area and about halfway along the southern side of Market Square. There were many outbuildings on the land behind the shops and cottages, including malt houses connected with some of the inns. Any of these could have been the starting point of the fire, but whatever the cause, it destroyed pretty much everything in the area and caused a total of £2,231 15s 8d. in damage.

The landowners took the opportunity of relocating their tenants further out of town by building replacement cottages along what we now know as North Street. For a long time afterwards the area was known as 'New Buildings'.

The hotel was demolished to make way for this Tesco store in 1965.

The damaged shops and premises on Market Square began to be replaced, though some quicker than others. The date stone on No. 30 Market Square shows that it was built in 1751. This may have replaced one of the fire-damaged properties, but that is quite a long time after the fire happened. It is, however, built in the then highly fashionable English bond checkerboard brick design, which would have been very expensive and certainly made a statement.

What didn't take quite as long to appear though was the Congregational Chapel, which was built on some of the cleared area of Water Lane in 1729. It also has the same checkerboard brick pattern on its front façade. The two side wings were added later to provide space for a vestry and schoolroom.

The Market End Inclosure Act (1758) ordered that the roads to Launton, Caversfield, Bucknell and Buckingham all be made 40 feet wide, but the condition of the roads is noted as having been 'very bad, almost impassable for a carriage'. However, the turnpike acts soon transformed the situation.

The road to Stratton Audley was turnpiked in 1768–69. The road to Aylesbury was turnpiked in 1770. The roads to Caversfield and Aynho (then both part of the coach road from London to Birmingham) were turnpiked in 1790–91. The road to Oxford was turnpiked in 1793. Toll houses in King's End, London Road and Crockwell monitored them all.

The Aylesbury and Aynho roads were made toll free by acts of 1875 and 1876, but the toll house on London Road was still standing well into the twentieth century, roughly

Bicester Congregational Chapel, photographed in the 1970s before it became a snooker club.

Bicester's first 'fire engine' was manufactured for the town by John Bristow, of London, around 1730, most likely to prevent the 1724 fire from happening again. It was restored in 2009 by Bicester Local History Society and is seen here next to its modern-day equivalent.

where Talisman Road is today. The toll house in Crockwell, located at the junction of Sheep Street, St John's Street and North Street, was demolished when the road was widened in the 1930s. In 1794 the King's End Inclosure Act was passed, with John Coker being the main allottee.

Stagecoaches began running between Bicester and London in 1752 and by 1795 there was a coach from Banbury to London passing through six days a week. There was also a stagecoach from Birmingham to London once a week, but by 1823 this had increased to two coaches running three times a week. A weekly stagecoach to Oxford began running on Saturdays in 1794 and a mail cart in 1798.

The London Road toll house, pictured in the 1950s.

The Crockwell toll house is on the right side of the road, where the two women are standing, pictured in 1910.

The building in London Road that we know today as Hometree House was originally called Bicester Hall. It was built in the early nineteenth century for an apothecary called Thomas Davis.

By 1874 it was in the hands of Baron Henry Schroeder, a London merchant banker of German descent, whose bank, Schroeders, still exists. He used Bicester Hall as a country retreat and hunting box.

By the end of the nineteenth century it was owned by Kenelm Charles Pepys, 4th Earl of Cottenham. He was Master of the Bicester Hunt between 1895 and 1899 and added the large brick-built stable block at the Victoria Road end of the property in 1896. He also had a covered entranceway added to the front of the house, which enabled visitors to get to and from their carriages without being exposed to the weather.

That was the last time the building was used as a single residence. During the First World War it was converted into a convalescent hospital under the Voluntary Aid Detachment of the Red Cross. It was initially under the command of Miss Esther Hendrick, daughter of Doctor Hendrick, who lived next to the hospital at No. 3 London Road. It had fifty-six beds for lower ranking soldiers from all regiments and was a hugely successful operation. It even produced its own monthly magazine, *Whizz-Bang!*, for a few years.

In 1919, the building was purchased by Oxfordshire County Council to house the County School, which opened in September 1924. The first headmaster was John Howson. Fees were 10 to 12 guineas a year and the school opened with forty-two pupils – twenty-eight boys and fourteen girls, with ten free scholarships.

Bicester Hall during its time as a Red Cross hospital during the First World War.

Hometree House as it stands today.

The number of pupils had risen to 113 by 1928, and 277 by 1956. By then the headmaster had a staff of thirteen full-time and two part-time teachers. They also had a sixth form with seventeen pupils. There were nine classrooms, a gymnasium, two laboratories, a woodwork room, dining room and kitchen. The school achieved grammar school status in 1946 and remained in the same building until it moved to a new site off Queen's Avenue in 1963.

After the school moved out the building was occupied by the Department of Health and Social Security. It was eventually sold by the council in 1986 and developed by McCarthy & Stone into retirement flats, when it was also renamed Hometree House.

The council retained some of the hall's grounds though, which is now occupied by the Bicester Community Support Service, and The Earl of Cottenham's stables now house Bicester Children and Family Centre.

The Bicester Hunt was founded in 1778 when John Warde bought a pack of hounds based on the main kennels at Bainton. It quickly became a popular pastime for the local gentry and traces of the hunt's influence over the local area can still be found today, such as the hunt symbols used on many local organisation badges and a few fox-shaped weathervanes in the town centre.

The first Master of the Bicester Hunt was Sir Thomas Mostyn in 1800. He purchased Swifts House, near Stoke Lyne, and built stables and kennels there. His monument to his faithful hound, Lady, still stands on the hill near Bainton today. Thomas Tyrwhitt-Drake was Master of the Hunt from 1829 to 1851, when the area associated with the hunt stretched to Daventry, Buckingham and Oxford. In 1855, the kennels and the Swift House buildings became inadequate to house the Bicester Hunt, and new quarters were built in Stratton Audley. In the 1870s the hunt was attracting high society, with frequent visits from royalty, dukes, ambassadors and aristocrats.

In the early 1900s there were many hunt-related activities in the area and people came to Bicester for the season. Special trains were put on to transport participants, staff and horses. Big houses were used as meeting points and hosted extravagant hunt-related social events.

With all this activity and celebrity, the associated industries and trades inevitably thrived. Blacksmiths, saddlers, tailors and stables all flourished in the town. Likewise, pubs and inns also benefited from the influx of people and money, particularly The King's Arms in Bicester and The Cartwright Arms in Aynho.

After the First World War, the Bicester hunting scene carried on much as it had done in the previous century. Hunting in Bicester was even depicted on cigarette cards. However, the war years of 1939–45 put a damper on the hunting scene and it fell to the more elderly of the population to keep things going. Mrs Margaret Lloyd-Mostyn, from Hethe, was well known for searching out extra food for the hounds.

In the 1950s and 1960s, there was a hunting revival attracting vast crowds. Hunts began to merge, and in 1986 the Bicester & Warden Hill Hunt amalgamated with the Whaddon Chase Hunt. In 2003, the now Bicester Hunt with Whaddon Chase was incorporated into a limited company, which still operates today.

In the late 1990s national controversy surrounding fox hunting had reached its peak, communities became passionately divided on the subject, and protestors became a part

A crowd gathers in Market Square to see the Boxing Day Meet of the Bicester Hunt in around 1910.

The Boxing Day Meet still attracted a crowd well into the 1980s.

of hunting events across the country. The Boxing Day assembly of the Bicester Hunt was a prime example of this, and costs for policing Market Square proved so high that the assembly of the hunt was forced to move to Launton.

In November 2004 Parliament passed an Act to ban fox hunting. So, drag hunting replaced fox hunting, and other riding activities began to occupy the hunt calendar. It is still a controversial subject, but there is no denying that the Bicester Hunt has played an integral and highly influential factor in the history of Bicester.

The King's Arms Hotel originally opened as a coaching inn in the sixteenth century. It was one of Bicester's two main inns and was the stopping point for stagecoaches for many years. In the nineteenth century it became the centre for the Bicester Hunt, for which horses could be hired or stabled in the yard at the back.

The façade we see today is not the original. Like many of the older buildings in the town it was given a facelift in the early nineteenth century, reflecting the town's prosperity and high aspirations. A lot of the Georgian stucco buildings in the town centre hide much older buildings behind their façades.

In St Edburg's churchyard there is an old weather-beaten headstone that is largely unreadable now but does bear the names of sixty-four people. The stone, with the names upon it, is a memorial to the victims of the cholera epidemic that scourged Bicester in 1832.

The outbreak led to the formation of a Board of Health, led by Viscount Chetwynd, who lived in Bicester House at the time. He quickly organised relief (the distribution of

Today's façade is not the original.

bread, meat, soup and brandy) and cleansing of the most affected areas (Crockwell and New Buildings being the most heavily hit), as well as speedy burial of the dead. But the outbreak still caused sixty-four deaths, that we know of, over a six-week period, a higher proportion of the population than recorded in any other town in England.

In those days medical and hospital services were practically non-existent, doctors and nurses were few, and the standards of public hygiene were generally low. People who contracted cholera died within a few hours. Terror quickly mounted in the town, and so did the death toll.

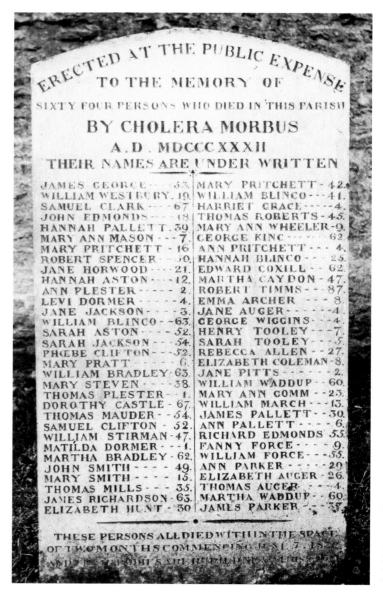

The marker for the mass grave no longer stands in its original location and is no longer as legible as it was here in the 1890s.

But the total of sixty-four deaths was nearly increased to sixty-five. A young boy named John Hudson fell ill with the disease. Barely more than a year old, he quickly collapsed into unconsciousness and was later certified as being dead by his doctor. The funeral arrangements were made by his family and the boy's body was placed in a coffin.

A few hours before the time fixed for the funeral, and before the undertaker had screwed down the coffin lid, the boy's grandmother bent down to kiss her grandson for the last time. She felt him move. Quickly the boy was lifted from the coffin and, as the hours passed, he showed further signs of being very much alive.

Subsequently young John Hudson made a complete recovery from the dreaded cholera and went on to live a full and active life. As a young man he entered domestic service and travelled hundreds of miles on stagecoaches. For nearly forty years he worked at Shillingford's brewery until the firm disbanded in 1891.

Apart from his remarkable escape during the epidemic, John Hudson was the first old-age pensioner in Bicester to receive his pension application form from the Post Office.

On 7 June 1909 John Hudson was struck down by a cerebral haemorrhage and died at his home in Manchester Terrace, Victoria Road. He was seventy-eight years of age.

5

Victorian Grandeur

One of the earliest directories of English workhouses, published in 1725, records that Bicester had a charity school whose pupils were employed in work as well as learning. The children were employed in spinning jersey. A weaver in the town supplied them with work and they were split into groups: six boys working one day, another six the next and so on.

This is the earliest reference to any kind of workhouse in the town, but by the time the parliamentary survey of poor relief was completed in 1777 Bicester had a parish workhouse in operation in London Road for up to forty inmates. In 1782 the inmates were employed in spinning wool, jersey and coarse linen.

In 1809 the overseeing of the workhouse was contracted out to Henry Chandler on a salary of £3 10s per week for up to twenty inmates, plus 3s 6d a week for each additional pauper. He lived in the workhouse and received an additional income from the inmates' work, in return for which he supplied them with food, clothing, accommodation and taught the children to read.

Labourers' wages were made up by the parish on a scale that was determined by the current price of bread. By 1820 the high price of bread following the introduction of the Corn Laws had pushed the poor rates to very high levels. Able-bodied paupers were sent around local ratepayers in the hope that they would provide them with work, a practice known as the 'roundsman system'.

In 1821, Sir Gregory Page-Turner offered to provide work for any unemployed paupers in his quarry and brickfield at Blackthorn. This scheme reduced the poor rate by half but was not a popular measure with the labourers in the town and, in 1826, resulted in a riot that destroyed the Town House and Shambles in Market Square.

In 1830 an emigration scheme was organised by the Bicester Emigration Committee to send some of Bicester's paupers to America. £1,000 was borrowed to fund the project and, on 24 May 1830, seventy-one adults and forty children set off for Liverpool. However, some of the prospective emigrants got cold feet on the way and returned to Bicester, where they again became a burden on the parish.

The Bicester Poor Law Union was formed on 1 August 1835 at the first meeting of the Bicester Board of Guardians, headed by Viscount Chetwynd. They were an elected body, forty members in total, representing the thirty-eight parishes that the Union covered. They had their first meeting at the Black Boy Inn, Market Square, and their first task was to replace the London Road workhouse with one large enough to serve the entire Union.

The new workhouse was built to the north-west of Bicester and opened in October 1836. It was designed to accommodate 350 inmates and cost a total of £4,640. This included an infirmary and a schoolroom.

Although everyone did whatever they could to stay out of the workhouse, for many of the poor who became sick or infirm, it was the only option. The Board of Guardians

The workhouse had a main central block with a wing on each side. One side is shown here and the front elevation is on the right of the image.

employed one of the doctors in the town to oversee the care of the poor, which included home visits for anyone receiving outside relief, but since the Union covered thirty-eight parishes it was often more practical to bring the sick to the infirmary.

A pest house had been built in Bicester after a large-scale outbreak of smallpox had started in 1752. This allowed for anyone with an infectious disease to be isolated from the general population while they were treated, and their property cleansed. But smallpox continued to be a problem for many years, particularly around Crockwell. By 1872 the

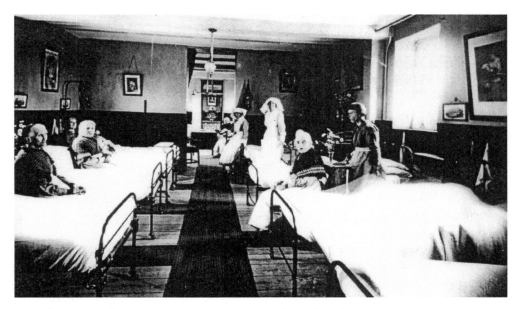

The infirmary ward in the workhouse seems to have always been busy.

pest house was no longer adequate, and an isolation hospital was proposed to be built next to the workhouse. This was built a few years later and consisted of three wards, one specifically for typhoid and another for scarlet fever.

The workhouse remained in operation until the Bicester Board of Guardians was disbanded in 1939. The workhouse then became, for a while, the Frank Gray Home for Boys, an institution aimed at saving the impoverished young from drifting into a life on the road.

After the Second World War the building was converted into flats and became known as Market End House. But the upkeep was too costly to maintain and so it was demolished in 1966, after a brief period of use by the county fire brigade for training crews in performing rescues from smoke-filled buildings. Market End Way now stands on the site.

Nos 6 and 8 Sheep Street, next to the White Hart public house, used to be the location of a long line of ironmonger shops. The business that would become Palmer Bros was initially opened there by Thomas Gibbs in the early nineteenth century, but the building is most likely to have been an ironmongers shop ever since it was built by the Burrows family in 1688. Gabriel and John Burrows both issued their own trade tokens in the 1660s and their family also had ironmonger's shops in Oxford and Thame.

Thomas Gibbs was later joined by his cousins, John and William Palmer, two of three brothers who together became one of the most successful trading families in Victorian Bicester. By the time of his death in 1877, William Palmer had amassed a fortune of almost £20,000. He held a controlling interest in the ironmongery business and was the managing director of the Bicester Gas Company. He and his wife, Elizabeth, were the original owners of the Garth, then known as the Poplars, and were probably the people who had the mansion built.

Unfortunately, construction finished too late for the couple to properly enjoy it as William died within a couple of years, and from William's death until her own in 1918, Elizabeth lived at Rose Cottage, a Victorian property that stood in its own grounds next to the London Road entrance to the Garth. She retained William's controlling interest in the ironmongery business after his death, but the day-to-day running of the business was taken over by William's nephews, William Gibbs Palmer and Edward Arthur Palmer.

Palmer Bros advertised themselves as 'general and furnishing ironmongers, cutlers, braziers, iron and tin plate workers, bell hangers, gas fitters, and agents for agricultural implements.' Their shop sold a variety of goods including lamps, ovens, cutlery, paint and petrol. They also acted for many years as agents for both Norwich Union fire and life insurance and the General Hail Storm Insurance Company, providing cover to farmers in the event of damage to their crops.

In 1910 Elizabeth sold the business to Charles Ashmore, who had been working for the company for many years by then. Originally from St Ives in Huntingdonshire, Charles moved to Bicester and married his wife, Priscilla, in 1882. They first lived in King's End, but they moved in over the shop when Charles brought the business and lived there together until Charles's death in 1928.

Outside Palmer Bros store in the early 1900s.

Their son, Robin, then took over the business and ran it until his death in 1943. He was then succeeded by his son, Roland and Roland's wife, Jean, who eventually passed it on to their two daughters, Mary and Pat. They then went on to run it together with Mary's husband, Clifford Carter, until the shop closed in 2006.

The original building was built in 1688, but the building that stands there today was built in 1969, after the original building burnt down. The fire engulfed the building during a snowstorm in the early hours of 20 February 1969. The heat of the fire was so intense that it melted the brass weights of the weighing scales and buckled Pyrex glass plates that were on display. To quell the fire the many fire crews in attendance had to lay an additional hose through Market Square to bring water from the open-air swimming pool near Causeway. According to a report in the *Bicester Advertiser*, smoke blanketed Sheep Street entirely and many residents had to be evacuated. The damage was estimated at the time at over £100,000.

Shortly after William Palmer's death in 1877, his wife, Elizabeth, sold the house they had just built, called The Poplars, and moved into Rose Cottage, a lodge by the main gates. Baron Adolf Deichmann, a London-based banker of German origin, purchased it from her, renamed it as the Garth, and made it into his hunting box. The popularity of the Bicester Hunt no doubt influenced his decision to buy the property.

When the baron became too old to hunt, he turned to four-in-hand coach driving and was reputed to have kept two teams of horses at the Garth for this purpose.

Garth House, as it appears today.

In 1891 the house and its 17-acre estate were sold to the Keith-Falconer family for £8,000. Charles Adrian Keith-Falconer, born in 1861, had married Williamina Emily Hume Dick in 1887 and they had one son, Adrian Wentworth Keith-Falconer, born in 1888.

Charles died in 1920, leaving Williamina a widow. During her time in Bicester Williamina became quite active in the Bicester Hunt and continued to ride with them, always side saddle, until well into her seventies, even though she was reputed to have broken every bone in her body in falls while riding with the hunt. This love of hunting, and her love of Old English sheepdogs, eventually led to the creation of one of the more curious features of Garth Park that we have today, in an area that Williamina herself referred to as the 'Garden of Peace'.

Hidden away in the trees, between the south lawn and the children's play park, you will find the graves of King John, King William, Queen Elizabeth, Prince Rupert and Lady Maud, all laying side by side with Isaac, Esau, Snip, Gipsy and Jaffa. Each grave has an elaborate headstone engraved with a fond tribute to the deceased and a classical quotation, but it is not a long-lost royal graveyard. They are all the graves of Williamina's pet dogs, apart from Jaffa, who was the family's pet cat. More impressive still are the two larger headstones nearby marking the graves of Carmelite and Don Quixote, again each carved with words of tenderness. These were two of Williamina's hunting horses.

Williamina continued to live in the Garth until her death there in 1945. The following year the house and gardens were purchased by Bicester Urban District Council, now

Right: Keith-Falconer coat of arms.

Below: Williamina's 'Garden of Peace'.

Bicester Town Council, for £6,500, largely due to the generosity of Lord Bicester, the Honourable Arthur Child Villiers, Major Adrian Keith-Falconer and Major Philip Fleming. The building and grounds were given to the people of Bicester and have been the council's base of operations ever since.

The building is a fairly modest version of the kind of Tudor Revival style that was all the rage in the Victorian period. The front façade has the outline of a sixteenth-century Tudor hall house with three projecting gables. Each of these has small decorative bands of faux black and white timber framing to the upper level. The right gable seeks to mimic a jettied building – very common in the Tudor period – and the oriel window in the central projection is a common Jacobean motif. The other decorative features are unmistakably Victorian. There are hanging fish scale tiles on some walls, machine-pierced bargeboards to the dormer windows and gables, and crested ridge tiles on the roof. At the rear of the building is a small round turret – expressing the romantic Victorian view of an Englishman's home being his castle.

Despite its continued occupation, over the latter years of the twentieth century the fabric of the building fell into disrepair and the top floor became unusable. In 2012 the building had to be re-roofed and in 2014 government grants were secured to bring part of the house up to modern standards of insulation and double glazing while preserving the period features.

An Englishman's home is his castle.

Apart from the pet cemetery and the bell mentioned earlier, various interesting artefacts can be found in the grounds today. The bandstand was originally erected in a suburb of Barnsley, but when it was taken down and sold as scrap it was purchased and renovated by Bicester Town Council. Another curiosity is the German telephone box that stands near the house's front entrance. It was donated to the town in May 1990 by Bicester's twin-town, Neunkirchen-Seelscheid.

Work on the Buckinghamshire Railway was started in 1848 by the London & North Western Railway. The first section of the line, Islip to Bletchley, was opened on 1 October 1850, which included a brand-new station in Bicester. At Bletchley the line linked to the main line from London Euston, and a temporary omnibus service completed the link from Islip to Oxford until the remainder of the line was opened on 20 May 1851.

In the lead up to the grand opening in October a committee was formed to arrange the town's celebrations. £90 was raised through a public subscription and the railway company laid on a special train for the occasion.

At 9:30 a.m. on 1 October an excursion train, carrying the committee and their friends, left Bicester to the cheers of the hundreds of people that crowded the station. They were welcomed into Islip station to the sound of 'See the Conquering Hero Comes' played by Adams' Oxford Brass Band. They stayed in Islip for lunch while the first ever passenger train left the station. Then they returned to Bicester, accompanied by the band who played a hearty tune along the way.

After they returned to Bicester at 1 p.m. everyone gathered with the poorer people of the town in the cricket field close to the station to have a celebration dinner. 1,000 lbs of meat and 200 loaves of bread were provided to feed the 900 men and women present,

Services from Bicester station proved very popular.

and 800 cakes and 12 gallons of currant wine were provided for the 800 children. The day ended with a great firework display in Market Square in the evening.

The railway was a great benefit to the town, but the following year, after the rest of the line to Oxford had opened, the people of Bicester came to realise just how dangerous it could also be.

On 6 September 1851 a special excursion train laid on for the Great Exhibition left Euston station carrying 200 passengers. At Bletchley the driver was told not to stop at Bicester but to carry on straight through to Oxford. However, no one told the stationmaster at Bicester about this. Expecting the train to stop he had the points switched to move the train over to the platform track.

When the train steamed through at full speed the points couldn't handle the force and the train was derailed. The first three coaches overturned and smashed to pieces, while the engine eventually came to rest about 2 feet from the stationmaster's house. It took three hours to rescue all the trapped passengers from the wreckage. Five people had been killed in the accident and Joseph Luckett, a cheesemonger from London, died from his injuries the following day.

An inquest was held on 15 September at the King's Head Inn, where the bodies of the six victims had been kept in a makeshift morgue. The stationmaster testified that, in his opinion, the train should've been able to safely, if uncomfortably, negotiate the points at speed. He suggested that some gravel or grit could've got between the points and stopped them engaging properly.

The inquest eventually ruled that several factors had come into play and the blame couldn't be traced to one specific fault. The jury decided that all trains should stop at Bicester until two tracks could be installed for the full length of the line.

The station changed its name to Bicester London Road in the 1950s to distinguish it from Bicester North. It continued to operate until passenger services were withdrawn in 1967, though the line remained open to goods traffic serving the nearby Army Ordnance Depot.

The station was reopened on 9 May 1987 when British Rail started a shuttle service between Bicester and Oxford. That's when the station was renamed Bicester Town. By then the station building had fallen into disrepair and the westbound platform had been demolished.

By the end of the century the station building had also been demolished. However, in 2008 plans were announced to rebuild the station as part of Chiltern Railways' new link to Oxford. This new station was named Bicester Village station, after the retail outlet it serves, and was officially opened on 26 October 2015.

One thing you can say about the Victorian people of Bicester is that they certainly knew how to get organised. In the space of about fifty years, they managed to bring in big improvements to transport, law and order, education, healthcare and recreation.

In 1857 the Police House in Church Street was built, only a year after the County & Borough Police Act (1856) made professional policing a requirement throughout the country. It was built by Thomas Jones, of Oxford, for £825 and initially it accommodated the town's earliest full-time professional police force of one inspector and five officers. By 1900 it was staffed by twelve officers, six covering the town and the rest covering the surrounding rural parishes.

The station was pretty much abandoned for twenty years and slowly fell into disrepair.

The Courthouse was built next door in 1873. It was in this building where the town's magistrates would sit in judgement of those criminal cases within their jurisdiction. Perhaps the most famous case was that of William Abel Ryder. He was a grocer with a shop in Causeway who, after losing two baby sons that had been vaccinated for smallpox, refused to have his newborn son, Edward, vaccinated. He was ordered to pay a fine of 10s and costs of 8s (which were paid by the Anti-Vaccination Society) and to have the child vaccinated within three weeks. He still refused the vaccination so for the next few months he kept getting called back and fined again until eventually the court gave up trying to enforce it.

In 1864 the County Courthouse in Sheep Street was built. This remained in use as a courthouse until the 1920s and since then has remained in the legal profession by being taken over as solicitors offices.

Before the Education Act of 1870, there was no national government funding of education. What schooling there was, was provided by a hodgepodge of local philanthropists, enlightened employers, and religious groups. Each of them had their own biased agenda.

One of the main religious educational groups was the 'National Society for Promoting the Education of the Poor in the Principles of the Established Church'. This society supported and organised funding campaigns for the building of so-called National Schools – which is where Bicester's first taste of a national education system began. They brought together the church schools and charity schools into one institution. The boys had previously been taught in a room within St Edburg's Church, the girls in a building opposite the church owned by the Coker estate, and the poorest boys in the Bluecoats School next to the vicarage.

The Police House, built in 1857.

The Church Street courthouse, built in 1873.

The building in Piggy Lane that was the home for many years of St Edburg's Church of England Primary School originally opened in 1858 as the Bicester National Schools. It was built in the Victorian Gothic Revival style, which sought to use all the key architectural motifs of medieval Gothic – like the arched windows and grotesques that can be seen all over the original structure. Thomas Nicholson, the building's architect, was following the lead of Augustus Pugin, who pioneered the style and believed that it would reawaken the moral authority of the high church – which had lain dormant from years of Nonconformism.

The original building was divided into two symmetrical halves to enable the teaching of boys and girls completely separately – even the playgrounds and toilet buildings were separate.

The architect's plan also shows long rows of benches in each teaching hall facing a single master's position. It is highly likely that, at least in its first few decades of operation, pupils were taught here by monitors (older children) in groups of twelve or so – passing on what they had learnt in turn to the youngsters. This system enabled larger class sizes with fewer teachers, and thus enabled cheaper primary education.

The youngest children were originally taught in separate, smaller classrooms. But as the town grew and attendance increased the existing building became too small to house all the children, so a new infant school was built in Crockwell to free up teaching space in the main schools. This was opened in 1869 and eventually developed into Brookside Primary School. The building still exists, next to the roundabout at the junction of Queen's Avenue and St John's Street, but it has since been converted into several private residences.

The name 'Bluecoats' came from the distinctive uniforms that the boys were supplied with.

The National Boys and Girls Schools were kept separate but run together.

Bicester National Infants School, now converted into several houses.

Interior view of the national schools.

With the increasing variety of faiths in the town, and the overcrowded state of St Edburg's churchyard, the authorities found themselves in need of new burial space. Land south of the churchyard was purchased from Jonas Paxton in the 1860s and a town cemetery was created. This included a small chapel, catacombs, designated areas for Catholics and Nonconformists, and an unconsecrated area for atheists and criminals. It was later expanded in 1901, the 1960s and 1980s. At some point before the 1960s expansion the catacombs were filled in and burials placed on top; this is the area behind the chapel that sits between two lines of trees.

In April 1882, Jonas Paxton donated a patch of ground by London Road for the building of a new church hall. The first stone of St Edburg's Hall was laid on the site by Baroness Schroder on 14 June 1882, and the whole construction was completed in time for it to be officially opened by the Countess of Jersey on 12 December 1882. It had a function room and an office on the ground floor and an assembly room on the first floor.

It served the community for many years until it was replaced by a new church hall, built in Old Place Yard, and opened by the Bishop of Oxford on 19 March 1968. This new building incorporated the old tythe barn that had been part of the priory. By the 1990s it became too expensive to maintain and so the structure was reverted to just the original barn building, which opened as the new church hall in 1992. The land where the 1960s building had been was sold off and Dove Court was later built on it.

Tubbs' Bank was founded in 1793 by Thomas and William Tubb, two grocers who came to Bicester from Oxford in the 1780s. The bank became the centre of Bicester's economy

The cemetery chapel was built to hold funeral services for those who didn't want to use St Edburg's Church, but these days it is just a site office and storeroom.

Today St Edburg's Hall is a commercial property with its interior long ago converted into office space.

for the whole of the nineteenth century and continued to be run by multiple generations of the Tubb family until it was sold to Barclays Bank in 1920. Barclays still occupy the same premises today.

Many members of the Tubb family were philanthropists, contributing a lot to the welfare of the poorer residents of the town. Thomas Tubb, one of the founders, was a feoffee of Bicester's Town Stock, a charity reputedly formed in the twelfth century for the relief of 'decayed tradesmen'. Thomas' grandson, George, contributed funds towards the building of the National Schools and regularly distributed coal to the poor in winter. George's nephew, Henry, the last of the family to run the bank, maintained six almshouses in Chapel Street and financed a soup kitchen that operated in St Edburg's Hall.

Exterior view of Barclays Bank in 1973.

Above: Tubbs' Bank issued their own notes and cheques up until 1918.

Left: Henry Tubb, pictured in his cricketing gear in 1899, lived in Chesterton Lodge.

6

A World at War

Mountain's chemist shop, in Sheep Street, opened in 1902 when John Thomas Mountain took over Sandiland's chemist shop.

John was born in Lincolnshire in 1868 and trained as a pharmaceutical chemist in the late 1880s before coming to Bicester. Over the years he instructed all five of his daughters in the business, but only Dorothy stayed on permanently. She eventually took over the business when John's health began to decline towards the end of his life in January 1940. He was noted for having a 'courteous bearing and kind attention to the minor ills and ailments about which it was his lot to encounter', and soon after opening the business he had already earned the respect and patronage of a large clientele.

Outside of work he was quite the sportsman and became involved in many things. As a young athlete he had won many trophies, and he also played football, cricket and hockey for Bicester and Caversham. Ever ready to assist in anything which would promote the

Mountain's chemist was located next to where Iceland supermarket is today.

John Thomas Mountain was born in Lincolnshire in 1868 and died on 9 January 1940.

interests of youth in Bicester, he and Doctor Montgomery were two of the main advocates of the need for a sports ground in the town in 1922. When the scheme was eventually launched in 1929 he was appointed a trustee of Bicester Sports Association.

As a keen rifleman who represented Great Britain in several international competitions, it is likely down to him that the Oxford Road Sports Ground once had a shooting range.

He was also a founder of the Bicester Social Club and held the position of chairman for several years. He was a member of the Horticultural Committee of the Bicester Show. He became a member of the Bicester Urban District Council in 1911 and was appointed chairman in 1918. He was a member of both the Bicester Feoffees and the Chamber of Commerce, and belonged to the Bicester Choral Society.

Alf Evans' department store once occupied Nos 34, 36 and 38 Sheep Street. It was located opposite Evans' Yard and first opened in early 1918. All types of clothing, shoes, haberdashery, toys, material and wool were sold there. Though if you talk to anyone who remembers the place then the main thing they recall is the intricate system of pipes that ran from each sales counter up to the cash office. Whenever you made a purchase your money and bill would be sent up in a pod and then a few moments later the pod would return with your change and receipt. This system remained in use right up until the department store closed in 1981.

It was a popular store, but it wasn't how Alf originally started his business. Robert Alfred 'Alf' Evans started his working life in 1890, at the age of twelve, when he began

The Bicester football team after winning the Chipping Norton Hospital Cup in 1925.

Bicester Rifle Club at the butts.

working in the grocery shop that his father, John Wesley Evans, opened at No. 40 Sheep Street in 1886. Then, in the early 1900s, he would walk to most villages in the area, and regularly cycled to London and back, to collect special orders for clothes, which he brought back in a basket. That kickstarted his own retail business.

The front of the department store, featuring its famous display arcade.

In 1902 he opened two shops, at Nos 29 and 31 Sheep Street, one either side of what would become known as Evans' Yard. The drapers shop was a thriving business for many years. Local women used to set aside a certain amount of wool and collect it periodically to knit clothes for their families. Nearly all jumpers were hand knitted in those days. He also supplied material for dressmaking.

After moving into the department store the company went in for promotions and advertising in a big way. They even staged fashion shows in the Methodist Hall in the 1950s and got their retail staff to model clothes for adverts.

The store was split over two floors and had two entrances. Between the two doors were three glass display cases that made up an arcade that Alf was very proud of and featured prominently in all his advertising at the time.

After Alf died in 1956 his son, John, took over the shop and it was reorganised. By 1965 the front doors had been moved forward to enclose the arcade and increase the interior space.

When John died in 1971 his son, Henry, became the third generation to run the business. But, in 1981, the department store closed, and the menswear section reopened in a new shop on Market Hill, where Hiltons shoe shop had been for many years and where Connell estate agents now stands.

The whole Evans family was a big part of Bicester's life throughout the twentieth century. Not just in their retail business and employment opportunities, but also in various social and charitable activities. Alf's wife, Nellie, even got involved in projects like the open-air swimming pool that opened in 1933, of which she was one of the driving forces.

The two shops, either side of what would become known as Evans' Yard, pictured in 1910. Alf is standing on the right side of the archway.

The London Road railway station was fine if you wanted to visit Launton, Islip, Buckingham, or any of the local halts, but the only way to get anywhere further afield by train was to travel on that line and change onto one of the main-line services at either Oxford, Bletchley or Verney Junction.

All that changed in the early 1900s when the Great Western Railway (GWR) came along. They had set up a partnership with the Great Central Railway (GCR) to build new lines out from London as far as Ashendon Junction, where the GCR were able to rejoin their own main-line north of Grendon Underwood. This work was completed in 1906 and left the GWR to continue towards their existing line at Aynho. So works continued and ultimately connected through to Banbury by 1910, when the first goods trains began running along the line on 10 April. The line was then fully opened to passenger traffic on 1 July, along with a shiny new station in Bicester, now known as Bicester North. This finally gave the town direct rail connections to London and Birmingham.

When opened, the station represented the last golden age of the railways before the First World War. Capacious platforms and buildings, good passenger facilities and ample shelter beneath a deep overhanging canopy. Between the platforms were four tracks, the platform lines being long loops to hold the slower traffic out of the path of the main lines that ran through the centre, for the new route was effectively going to be the new GWR main line to Birmingham.

The first express train through Bicester GWR station on opening day, 1 July 1910.

However, the GWR were initially reluctant to stop trains at the new stations (Blackthorn, Bicester, Ardley and Aynho Park) as they were determined to compete with the LNWR's two-hour express London to Birmingham service. The compromise they came up with was to introduce slip coaches, where the express trains from Paddington would detach their rear coach as they approached the station and leave it behind to slowly coast to a stop. This happened at Bicester, where a local engine would then pick up the coach and bring it into the platform, then take it on up the line to drop passengers off at the next few stations.

The slip coach service continued to operate until 1960 when, at 6.12 p.m. on 9 September, the very last slip coach to operate in Britain was released from the express just after it passed Blackthorn and coasted gently on to be picked up and brought into Bicester North station for the last time. By then the line had already entered decline. Blackthorn station had closed in 1953, then, following Dr Beeching's 'Reshaping of British Railways' report, Ardley and Aynho Park stations closed in 1963 and all the main line London to Birmingham services were eventually switched back to the old route through Didcot and Oxford, with the last main-line service through Bicester running on 6 March 1967.

After that, work began on converting the line from Princes Risborough to Aynho over to a single track, closing the signal boxes at Bicester and Ardley and making one of the platforms at Bicester completely redundant.

Under British Rail, Bicester North remained largely forgotten. But the present-day role of Bicester North is quite different. In 1996, following the privatisation of British Rail, the line was taken over by Chiltern Railways. The line was then converted back to dual tracks and has seen a peak of over fifty trains a day run to London – a far cry from the five a day that ran when the line first opened a century earlier.

The station has been refurbished a few times since then. Most noticeably in 2011 when the tracks were realigned to allow for higher speeds, meaning that the London bound platform had to be widened quite considerably.

In 1887, to commemorate Queen Victoria's Golden Jubilee, the Horse & Groom public house, on Banbury Road, was purchased and converted into a nursing home. In 1904 it was noted as being 'quite one of the best institutions in Bicester'.

'It has two very nice little wards with three beds, which can be had on a small weekly payment. They have been found very useful in the case of men or women in service or in lodgings who have been taken ill or met with an accident and also in the case of country patients who need to be within easy reach of their doctor. Ever since 1887 the people of the parish, the poorer without payment and others with graduated payments, settled by the committee, have received its benefits.'

However, when the Great Western Railway came through Bicester, their planned route ran so close to the nursing home that it would be buried under the embankment. So the GWR bought the property for £1,000 and a site was found to build a new nursing home in King's End.

The Banbury Road nursing home shortly before it was closed.

The land for the new nursing home was leased from Colonel L. E. Coker for £1 per annum, and the building cost £1,100 to construct (the other £100 being donated by the Earl of Jersey). It was built by Thomas Grimsley, later of Grimsley & Sons, who was a prominent local builder and townsman. The first patients were admitted in September 1908 and cared for by Miss Goodwin and Nurse Plater, who had previously run the old nursing home.

In 1918, Major Lewis Aubrey Coker donated the freehold of the land to the hospital, in honour of the men and women of Bicester who had served in the First World War. Then a large donation was made in 1927 when Margaret Tubb, the widow of Henry Tubb, funded an extension to house a new ward and nurses' room in his memory.

In 1928 the hospital was registered as a nursing home and run as a cottage and community hospital for maternity use only.

With the creation of the National Health Service in 1948, the hospital became administered by Banbury & District Hospital Management Committee. In 1958 an extension was built by Ron Price to accommodate additional wards. During the 1970s, the purpose of the hospital changed from maternity to general nursing, mainly for elderly patients. An extension was built for Day Care, sponsored by the hospital's League of Friends, with money raised through various events. In 1974 the responsibility for the hospital's administration passed to Oxfordshire Area Health Authority.

In 1981 a physiotherapy room, donated by Iris Mackenzie, was added and an extension for the X-ray Department was built by the generosity of the people of Bicester.

Eventually though, the hospital building was no longer fit for purpose. In 2012 plans were approved to sell the building and its land and replace it with a new community

The King's End nursing home when it first opened in 1908.

hospital, built on land in Coker Close. Construction started in June 2013 and the new hospital first started taking in patients on 11 December 2014. It was then officially opened in July 2015.

During the First World War Bicester played its part just like every other town in the country. Recruiting offices were set up and many local men joined up to serve their country. A lot of them would never return.

Bicester Hall was converted into a Red Cross Hospital for the duration of the war. Many local people got involved in whatever way they could – some organised knitting groups to send socks and balaclavas out to our troops, others raised funds to help support the Red Cross.

Then, in 1918, Bicester Aerodrome opened as a Royal Flying Corps training ground. Later to become RAF Bicester, it was the first sign of Bicester becoming a garrison town.

Bicester Ordnance Depot opened in 1941, at the height of the Second World War. Its central location and convenient rail links made it one of the armed forces' major supply bases throughout the war. It continued to grow over the following decades and became so large that a whole housing estate in King's End had to be built just to accommodate the civilian staff.

Methodism began in Bicester in 1814 when Mrs J. Bowerman was 'awakened' while listening to the preaching of John Wesley at Brackley. She and her husband soon arranged

The Community Hospital in 2009, just a few years before it was closed.

The new Community Hospital building in Coker Close.

Bicester's Red Cross fundraising group during the First World War, including Revd Walter O'Reilly, the vicar of St Edburg's Church.

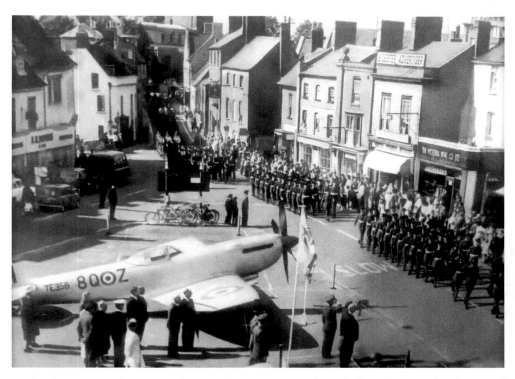

Battle of Britain Parade in 1962. The aircraft is an LF.16 Spitfire, which used to stand at the gate of RAF Bicester.

The Remembrance Day service in November 1928.

Bicester's war memorial was erected in
St Edburg's churchyard in 1921.

for the Brackley minister to visit Bicester and a room in their farmhouse was opened by
Mr Bowerman for these services.

Over the following years two separate branches of Wesleyanism developed in the town.
One stayed on the site of the farmhouse and eventually built Wesley Hall there.

The other branch bought a site in North Street and built a chapel there in 1840. Some
forty years later a schoolroom was added. In 1892 the chapel was enlarged, reseated and a
gallery added at a cost of £438. In 1904 an organ was installed costing £270.

The two separate churches eventually outgrew their buildings and came together to
build one common place of worship. Much of the site of their new church was bought in
1919, but the remaining property was purchased in 1925 after the North Street chapel was
sold. It was bought by the Jersey Lodge of Masons and became the Masonic Weyland Hall.

The Wesley Hall in Sheep Street continued to be used as a church until the new one
was built, after that it was used as a church hall and for the Sunday school until a new hall
was built behind the new church. Wesley Hall was then sold in 1955 to Woolworths. It
later became Coxeters furniture store and is now Home Comforts.

The new church was originally named the Grainger Hargreaves Memorial Church in
memory of a former, noted minister. Revd Grainger Hargreaves had been a missionary
in China, a minister in Australia and New Zealand and eventually chairman of Oxford
Methodist District for eighteen years. He had returned to Bicester in 1921 and died in
1923. Today though it is simply Bicester Methodist Church.

Bicester Methodist Church in Sheep Street.

The new church cost £7,000, including the purchase of the land. When the stone-laying ceremony was held on 23 September 1926, the first stone to be laid was in memory of Revd Grainger Hargreaves. On 23 June 1927 the new church was opened by Mrs J. Vanner Early, of Witney.

In 1942 a two-manual organ by Albert Keates of Sheffield was installed as a gift from Mr George Layton, one of the church's main benefactors. The organ is believed to have come from a bombed church. Mr Layton was organist for fifty years and he had opened the first garage in London Road in Bicester in 1910.

The Red Rhythmics Harmonica Band was founded by Sid Hedges, the local author and noted historian, best known for his chronicle *Bicester Wuz a Little Town*, in the 1930s and it ran successfully until the early 1950s. They wore red berets, white shirts and grey flannels, and Sid would often appear as conductor wearing a full evening suit.

The band played most of their concerts at towns in the region and at major halls in London, including the Royal Albert Hall. They also appeared several times on radio, usually from the BBC studios in Birmingham, and on television. Their fame led to the *Picture Post* magazine featuring an article on the church Sunday school under the headline 'Sunday School is Different Here'. Sid was also Sunday school superintendent for fifty years, following on from his father, George Hedges.

In the 1920s, as the population continued to grow and more and more cottages fell into disrepair, the council realised that a new housing estate was needed. A site between

The foundation laying ceremony for the new church.

The Red Rhythmics Harmonica Band, pictured in 1957.

Bucknell Road and the Workhouse was chosen and building work started in 1931 for what would be known as Highfield.

Bucknell Road already existed, and a lane called Facey's Road (what is now the northern half of George Street) ran from it down to the Workhouse. The first phase of construction

Sunday school pupils and staff in 1961.

Bucknell Road. These were some of the first houses to be built at Highfield.

began at the northern point where these two roads met and moved southwards along each road. The second phase, built in 1932, added The Oval to complete the triangle. From there works continued moving southwards.

The estate didn't originally have any street names, but it included what we know now as George Street, The Oval, West Street, East Street, The Approach, The Crescent, and part of Bucknell Road. When Market End House was demolished in 1966 Hudson Street was built to rehouse the residents.

All the houses were built to the same two or three standard designs and all the windows and doors were painted the same colour, so every street had a uniform appearance. A council surveyor would come around regularly to make sure that everything was being well maintained and kept up to standard.

When the Grammar School moved to Queen's Avenue, Highfield School was opened behind it, accessed from George Street. Eventually the two schools would be combined to form what we know of today as The Bicester School.

The idea of constructing a purpose-built pool was first mooted in the 1920s and then adopted in 1933, partly to provide work for several unemployed men during the Depression. The land already belonged to the Urban Council and the project cost a total of £986, £600 of which made up wages of the workforce. £400 had been raised by loans from the trustees and the remainder was collected from various fundraising events. Work started on 27 March 1933, but fundraising continued until well after the opening, including an ox roast in November 1935.

As shown here in the 1970s, the standards and uniform appearance were maintained for many years.

The committee in charge of building the pool are seen here visiting the site during construction.

On 29 June 1933 Mrs Tubb officially opened the newly built open-air swimming pool behind Bridge House, where the car park behind NatWest bank is today, at the end of Causeway.

Under the bright sunshine on that first day the emerald-green water and gleaming white walls proved to be most inviting and soon swimmers of all ages had lined up along one side of the pool, ready to take the first plunge. About 808 people attended the event, and lots were drawn to determine who should be the first two to enter the water and receive a prize of ten shillings each. The lucky winners were Leading Aircraftman Harris, from RAF Bicester, and Mr Victor Schafer, of Grendon Underwood. On the signal from Mrs Tubb they both dived into the water at the deep end (Mr Schafer still fully dressed, complete with a silk top hat!), immediately followed by another fifty swimmers.

We know it wasn't the first public pool in the town because John Dunkin's history of the town states that in the eighteenth century a wool comber constructed one in St John's Street. But a cottage was eventually built on it and, for many years, the closest thing Bicester residents had to a lido was a disused quarry just off the Bucknell Road.

The new public pool proved so popular that even the unsanitary conditions and primitive facilities didn't put people off using it. The changing hut had no roof on it so,

All in at once on opening day.

The changing facilities were notoriously simplistic, but at least they had a roof originally.

although it was private, you were always at the mercy of the weather. And as the pool water was only replaced at the start of each season (by the fire brigade) come September you could always find moss and algae growing around the edges and floating in the freezing cold water. The pool remained in use until the Bicester and Ploughley Sports Centre was opened on 7 March 1970.

The Regal Cinema opened in London Road on 1 September 1934 with a showing of Jack Buchanan in *That's a Good Girl*. A large art deco-style building designed by Birmingham based architect Harold Seymour Scott, it was originally operated by Union Cinemas, but in October 1937 it was taken over by Associated British Cinemas (ABC).

Despite the large size of the building, it only had one screen and all the seating was on a single floor – no private boxes or upper circle for Bicester. For 1s you could sit at the front and crick your neck trying to see the screen, the seats behind those were 1s 9d, and then the ones behind those were 2s 9d.

From 1968 it became a part-time bingo hall, and on 3 December 1975 the last film was shown, Paul Newman in *The Towering Inferno*. It was then taken over by Zetters Enterprises and became a full-time Zetters Bingo Club, until it closed in 1987. The building was demolished in 1988 and a block of flats, named Regal Court, was built on the site.

Seen here around 1970, for many years it served as both a cinema and bingo hall.

7

Into the Atomic Age

By the 1930s it became apparent that, thanks to the increase in both the volume and size of traffic flowing through the town, that the existing road layout was not adequate. It was decided to reopen the old route from King's End to Crockwell, the first time this has been open to road traffic since 1790.

Work began in laying the new road, but when the Second World War broke out, the project had to be put on hold. So, although the road was built in the 1930s, it wasn't officially opened until the late 1940s. Initially it was called New Road, but then it was decided to name it Queen's Avenue in honour of Queen Elizabeth II's coronation in 1953. Trees were planted along the sides of the road as part of this commemoration, each one

Today Queen's Avenue is one of the busiest roads in the town.

donated by a different local organisation. They originally had plaques at the base of each tree to show who had donated it.

Ploughley Rural District Council then went on to purchase land along the north side of the road, from the Coker estate, to build their new offices in Waverley House, later to become the magistrates' court, as well as new police, fire and ambulance stations.

After the Second World War the new Labour government, through Oxfordshire County Council, compulsorily purchased a large area of Home Farm land to provide council houses on what we now know as the King's End estate, providing homes for workers imported from the north of England and Scotland to be employed at Bicester Ordnance Depot. There were also private plots made available for individuals to build their own homes.

This was later followed by the Churchill Road estate in the 1960s, with its roads named after Oxford colleges: Glory Farm (aircraft), Greenwood (rivers) and King's Meadow (authors) in the 1980s; Southwold (trees), Langford Village (birds) and Bure Park (plants) in the 1990s; Kingsmere (racecourses) and Elmsbrook (fruit and vegetables) in recent years.

On Easter Monday 1962 a large and excited crowd gathered in the town centre to witness a pram race. Organised by the Bicester Round Table, it was a charity event that received so much support that it went on to become an annual event for many years.

The *Bicester Advertiser* reported after the first event that it was 'a tremendous and boisterous success, as competitors, sporting flamboyant hats, dressed in fantastic infants clothes and sucking succulent dummies and bottles, drew loud peals of laughter and delight from the thronging people surging in their hundreds down Sheep Street.'

An astounding assembly of bizarre prams was lined up. Some were donated, some borrowed, and others taken out of ditches. Mr F. T. J. Hudson started the race in Bell Lane with a resounding shot from his starting pistol. The eager sportsmen rushed for their

One of the races in the 1970s.

ancient vehicles; a few with the swiftness of deer, but many with the steady, measured gait of carthorses.

Collisions and breakdowns occurred early in the race with pram wheels buckling under the weight of their 'babies'. Other competitors were pitched out of their prams and sent sprawling along the road. The teams careered down Sheep Street, stopping at five pubs on the way to drink beer placed on tables outside. After looping around Market Square, they returned up Sheep Street towards the finish line.

Messrs Pat Smith and Edward Shaw, representing the White Lion, passed the winning line first, having completed the course, and all the drinking, in five minutes and forty-four seconds. For their efforts they won a trophy and four and a half gallons of beer!

In total, twenty-four teams entered that first competition, and things went from strength to strength in subsequent years.

On Monday 10 May 1965 people came from miles around and gathered for hours in the town centre, waiting for the visit of Her Majesty, Queen Elizabeth II, and His Royal Highness Prince Philip, the first time on record when a reigning monarch had officially visited the town.

Flags and bunting hung all around Market Square and shop window displays were all decorated in red, white and blue. Students and employees had taken the day off specially

The Queen arrives in Market Square.

People gathered to get a good view from any vantage point.

and the atmosphere of excitement and anticipation was palpable. As the royal party arrived, the crowd surged forward, flag waving and cheering. The upper-floor windows in many of the buildings around the square were occupied with people bunched tightly together, all eager to get a good view of the proceedings. There were even a few brave souls who scaled the roofs of some buildings just to get a look.

The visit started at Bicester Central Ordnance Depot where, at 11 a.m., the Queen received the Royal Salute from the Guard of Honour mounted by the 46 Bn. RAOC. Then, riding in an open Land Rover, the Queen was given a tour of the depot, which was undergoing a £2.5-million redevelopment at the time.

The royal party then proceeded through Ambrosden, where the roads were lined by military families and schoolchildren, and on to Graven Hill, where displays of service clothing, firefighting equipment and air drop equipment were exhibited. Prince Philip closely inspected the 20 lbs of metal left from guns used in the Crimea War, which is now used for the manufacture of the Victoria Cross. Then the depot visit ended with a stop at the Officers' Mess.

The royal car arrived in Market Square a few minutes later than expected. It had been previously announced that the Queen and Prince Philip would not have time to speak with the councillors who were presented, but, to the delight of the huge crowd, the schedule went by the wayside and the royal visitors chatted and joked with fifty councillors and senior officials. Prince Philip made another of his light-hearted comments, to ease the strain of the long line of handshakes, when he asked Councillor Mears, a railway engine driver, 'What happened to the tea making since the changeover from steam to diesel?' Councillor Mears' reply is not recorded.

The Queen and Prince Philip then signed portraits of themselves, which were to be hung in the council chambers of both Bicester and Ploughley Councils. They also signed the visitors' books for both councils.

The final stage of the royal visit was lunch at RAF Bicester. Leaving Market Square the royal car drove slowly along Sheep Street and St John's Street, where the gathered crowd of schoolchildren from Bicester and some of the local villages waved their Union Jacks and cheered as the royal party drove by.

The pen used by the Queen to sign her portrait for Bicester Urban District Council was presented to the town by Mr F. T. J. Hudson JP, Chairman of the Bicester Magistrates. Prince Philip used his own pen, remarking that he did not like using any other.

The earliest records of any Catholicism in Bicester since the Reformation date back to 1869, when small services began being held in a cottage in Sheep Street, where Diamond Villa now stands. The Catholic church in Hethe oversaw the services.

As the community grew, they raised the funds to build a schoolroom in King's End, where Montgomery House Surgery is today.

This opened in 1883 to educate the Catholic children of the town, but also provided a larger space for the church services. Services were held there until 1908 when the nuns living in Priory House opened part of their chapel for public use.

When the nuns left Bicester in 1920 the whole chapel became available to the public. But the congregation continued to grow and by the 1960s the chapel was no longer adequate. In 1961 Bonner's stables in Causeway were purchased and the land cleared. A new parish church was designed by Desmond Williams & Associates and Norman Collison & Son, builders of Bicester, were then brought in to construct it. The Church of Our Lady of the

The school building on Piggy Lane.

Inside the school, boys and girls were taught together.

The Chapel (Near view). The Priory. Bicester, Oxon.

The chapel interior as it was in around 1910.

The new Catholic church was undoubtedly a modern build, but tried to be in keeping with its surroundings.

Immaculate Conception was then officially opened by the Archbishop of Birmingham on 23 March 1963. The final cost of the church was £43,000, with an additional £10,000 for furnishings.

The statue above the main entrance was replaced in 1993 with the bronze statue by Mark Delf of Stafford that still stands there today, but otherwise the exterior wasn't changed much until the John Paul II Centre was built on the side the church in 2010. This was opened on 9 December 2010.

It is somewhat ironic to think that, when the Town Council was trying to find ways of easing congestion in the town centre in the 1970s, the best solution they could come up with was to build a relief road that basically followed the same route that the town's very first road had followed between Crockwell and St Mary's Bridge, a route that had been abandoned many centuries earlier. It meant knocking down properties at either end, but Manorsfield Road was built in the early 1970s and opened to traffic in 1976.

Mark Delf's bronze statue is still a prominent feature of the front façade today.

The Market Square entrance to Manorsfield Road, seen here in 1974 before the road was fully open.

The original plan was to build another relief road from London Road to Chapel Street (basically where Saxon Court is today) and upgrade the top end of Chapel Street so that the town centre could be bypassed altogether. This would allow them to pedestrianise Sheep Street and Market Square and generally improve the town centre. Unfortunately, only the Manorsfield Road section of the plan was completed. Sheep Street was later pedestrianised, in 1994, but with traffic still flowing through Market Square the vision of a car-free town centre never came to pass.

8

The Town of Today

Crown Walk was opened on 26 November 1988 with a huge fanfare and big opening ceremony, complete with clowns, jugglers and a balloon race. Rod Hull and Emu were invited along to cut the ribbon, much to the delight of the local children.

Together with the other shopping arcades in the town, such as Evans' Yard, Wesley Lane, and Dean's Court, Crown Walk was seen to bring Bicester's shopping facilities to a more competitive level against other Oxfordshire towns.

The architecture and overall design of the precinct differed a great deal in style from the rest of Bicester's town centre. Mainly because, unlike the other lanes, passageways and yards that had been developed before, the planners did not have to adapt their plans to accommodate existing buildings, cottages or workshops. At the Market Square end they knocked an archway entrance through the old Cross Keys pub, and at the Sheep Street end they completely replaced the 1960s building that had itself replaced the Crown Hotel (the hotel being where the name 'Crown Walk' came from). Between those was open space and they were free to do whatever they wanted.

Bicester Village pulls in millions of visitors each year from all over the world.

Originally there were twenty-three shops, ranging from florists and jewellers to bakers and a travel agent. These retailers have changed over time, but its central location has always made it more popular than other shopping arcades around the town centre. In 2016 it was incorporated into the Pioneer Square development, but it has still suffered in recent years with the general decline of the high street in favour of online shopping.

Bicester Village first opened on 26 April 1995 and initially attracted over 4 million visitors a year. It has grown a lot since those early days and now boasts over 150 shops, all bringing over 7 million visitors to the area each year, according to 2019 figures.

The biggest change to the town centre in recent years was the construction of Pioneer Square. Spearheaded by Sainsbury's as an attempt to muscle in on Tesco's longstanding monopoly, the development also incorporated several shops and restaurants, as well as a cinema (the first cinema in Bicester since the Regal closed in 1975).

Bicester's population is increasing now more rapidly than it has ever done before. And with the expanding population comes the need for more employment and more goods. This is reflected in the new shopping precincts and the larger number of retail service outlets. Town centre developments like Crown Walk, the pedestrianisation of Sheep Street, and Pioneer Square have all come about because of this.

The difficulty the town centre seems to be facing at the moment is that anything that can be done online can be done a lot cheaper, so high street retail space is no longer affordable for many companies. This means the town centre is slowly becoming a collection of bars, food outlets, hairdressers, and empty shops. At the same time the population continues to expand with more and more housing estates swallowing up the countryside.

In the face of such growth, it becomes even more important to preserve the rich heritage we have. The fact that this book exists at all is a testament to people's interest in the history of our town, and many local organisations, like Bicester Local History Society, work to promote and celebrating the town that Bicester used to be. The town has always evolved to meet the needs of the population without losing sight of its past, and will continue to do so for many years to come.